"One of the key sins of the University of Kentucky has been its own failure in recognizing, admitting, and showcasing the historical trials, tribulations, and accomplishments Black athletes endured during the early days of segregation and integration into the university's history; especially as it pertains to the University of Kentucky's athletics history with Black athletes. So many of these stories about the struggles that Black athletes had early in history at UK have not been told, and we are into the second decade of the twenty-first century. This book uncovers another one of those untold stories of the struggles of an early Black pioneer athlete that had to cross over and endure the racial barriers at UK and in his life—from his youth in his small hometown in Hastings, Florida, all the way through his life living in America trying to achieve the elusive "American Dream" for a Black man."

 —Rufus Friday, former publisher of the *Lexington Herald-Leader,* 2011 – 2018

"Derrick was so outstanding during his time at the University of Kentucky. You talk about being a leader. He was that and more for our team. When he called a play, we all knew damn well that was the right play… I love Derrick like my son. Today, he's still a dominant figure in the state of Kentucky. Even during his playing days, he was always looking toward the future, and he had such a keen business mind. As an athletics director and as a cabinet secretary, he managed and hired the right people to get the job done. I thought he could have been a congressman. He could still be one today if he wanted to. Because of all he's accomplished both on and off the field for the state of Kentucky, he will never be forgotten."

 —Fran Curci, University of Kentucky head football coach, 1973 – 1981

"When Derrick came on with the Raiders, everyone was impressed with his size, height, and his football credentials. But what really stood out was his great talent. Plus, he was super intelligent. You only had to tell him something one time, and he would get it. He never missed anything on the field and showed an exceptional a??i?? ' for playing the game. That translated to him ni?l?i? ?re and all the stuff about the game so qu

 —Raymond Chest? tate business partner

"Derrick had so many leadership qualities off the field. I used to call him a politician. I'm not surprised he ended up doing all those things he did after football. Even as a young person, Derrick was like an old soul in the way he addressed things and talked to folks. He was always straight up with all the players and coaches on the team. With Derrick, it was never about himself. It was always about doing positive things in the community. He always looked for ways to help others. He'd take younger players under his wing and give them direction. Life's not just about ourselves but also about those coming behind us. I really respected and looked up to him in that regard."

—Art Still, high school and college teammate, consensus UK All-American, NFL All-Pro

"I'm very proud of Derrick. He's done a fantastic job with not only his life in sports but also with his personal life. In everything he does, he's always trying to get to the next level. There's nothing he thinks that he can't do. Our parents instilled that type of thinking in all of us from the very beginning. Remember this: in everything you do, you're representing the family."

—Tyrone Ramsey, older brother No. 1/former high school principal

"So much of who Derrick is—and who we all are—comes back to what our parents instilled in us. It also comes down to the relationships you've developed with people across the years. You always want to remember where you came from and all the people who helped you along the way. You'll soon discover that Derrick's exactly that kind of guy."

—Robert Ramsey, older brother No. 2/former Kentucky Secretary of Personnel

"Derrick was always a good student. He always had his homework done, and when he came to school, he was always dressed well and looked like a top-notch student. I knew he was headed for something special."

—Ethel McNeil, former high school English teacher

"Even though Derrick was a star athlete, he would always take time out with the younger kids to encourage them. He was very comfortable speaking with everyone. When we had to make speeches in high school, Derrick pulled it off with ease. You saw back then that he was going to be a great leader."

—Al Carter, childhood friend and classmate

"Derrick led by example. Anyone could talk a good game, but the bottom line is playing the game. Derrick certainly did that. When he did a double-clutch dunk, or smacked somebody's jump shot into the bleachers, or threw a football the length of the football field, that's all we needed to see."

—Ken Fisher, high school teammate

"I think being a natural leader was the reason Derrick became so set on playing quarterback. We wanted all our players to respect the quarterback position. As a coach, I was demanding on Derrick. But I was demanding on everyone—including the athletes that went before him. The quarterback had so many responsibilities. I wanted to make sure Derrick was adequately prepared to handle anything that came his way. I wasn't about to let him slack off. If you get to be the quarterback, you must act like the quarterback. Not only on the field but in the community as well."

—Coach Andy Hinson, high school head coach

"My first engagement with Derrick happened at a military exercise we had at Fort Knox. His presence stood out immediately. It seemed everyone wanted to follow him when we went out on these military exercises because he always seemed to know what he was doing. He was an inspiration to many of those who were in our unit. I noticed that in every single one of his [future] endeavors—whether as a quarterback, as an athletics director, or as a cabinet secretary—Derrick exhibited the same traits that I remember made him so impressive and successful as a cadet."

—Major General Reuben Jones, United States Army Retired

"As African American men living out our lives, we're called to represent as role models. It's not just about what we're doing currently but also about what we're leaving behind for people who might not ever meet us or know us. This is what Derrick's entire memoir is about. It's a legacy of leading and living."

—Dr. Aaron Thompson, President of the Kentucky Council on Postsecondary Education

"Derrick could make friends with whoever he came in contact with. His leadership was about inspiring others and leading by example in order for everyone to reach a common goal. In 1974, he brought a winning attitude to the entire team. He was someone who encouraged and enabled people to reach their full potential while providing the needed support every step of the way. The guy was always positive, optimistic, and respectful to his teammates and coaches."

—Jerry Blanton, college teammate, former deputy commissioner of Kentucky state parks

"I was very familiar with Derrick's football career at the University of Kentucky and then in the NFL. That experience on the field transferred over to his other successes. He's a natural leader. He communicates in a way that people—his staff, people in the general assembly, people in higher education, employers—can understand. He's then able to get buy in from all the critical stakeholders."

—Scott Brinkman, former Kentucky executive cabinet secretary under Governor Matt Bevin

They Call Me Mr. Secretary
-Through the Lens of a Winner-

Derrick Ramsey

with Dr. John Huang

Foreword by Jim Host

Cover Photo: Derrick Ramsey/Kentucky Cabinet of Education and Workforce Development

Back Cover Kentucky Football Photo: Sports Illustrated
Back Cover NFL Photo: New England Patriots

Cover Design: Greg Gerlach

ISBN 9798860684300

First Printing 2023

This book is part memoir. It reflects the author's present recollection of experiences over time. Although the author has made efforts to ensure that the information in this book was accurate at press time, the author acknowledges that errors or omissions can occur. The author does not assume, and hereby disclaims liability to any party for any loss or damage caused by errors or omissions, whether such errors or omissions result from negligence, accident, or any other cause.

"There are no secrets to success. It is the result of preparation, hard work, and learning from failure."
    —Colin Powell

"Whenever men and women straighten their backs up, they are going somewhere, because a man can't ride your back unless it is bent."
    —Martin Luther King Jr.

"The greatest leader is not necessarily the one who does the greatest things. He is the one who gets the people to do the greatest things."
    —Ronald Reagan

"But there will come a time and a place to give back, and each individual will recognize that time and place."
    —Vernon Jordan

"The measure of who we are is what we do with what we have."
    —Vince Lombardi

"Don't worry about the horse being blind, just load the wagon."
    —John Madden

"Just win, baby!"
    —Al Davis

Contents

Foreword by Jim Host   x

Prologue   1

Chapter 1—Hastings, Florida   4

Chapter 2—Camden, New Jersey   30

Chapter 3—University of Kentucky   51

Chapter 4—NFL   90

Chapter 5—Life After Football   110

Chapter 6—Mr. Secretary   136

Chapter 7—What's Next?   151

Epilogue   158

Dr. John Huang—In His Own Words   160

About the Authors   162

To my parents

Foreword
By Jim Host

One of the University of Kentucky's greatest football teams ever was its 1977 edition which went 10 – 1. Curci's Cats, as they were called, were led by one of UK's best athletes of all time—Derrick Ramsey.

No one—and I mean no one—has ever been a better leader than Derrick. On the field, the guy simply refused to lose.

However, this book is about much more than just his football exploits. Even after his storied college and NFL career ended, Derrick continued serving his adopted state of Kentucky as secretary of two major cabinets in state government. He would then also go on to serve his beloved alma mater as a member of the UK Board of Trustees.

I've known Derrick since he first stepped on the turf at UK. We became very close friends after he returned to work with me on the UK TV Network as a color analyst. I'd listen to Derrick on those football broadcasts and found him to be extremely knowledgeable. But I couldn't understand how a guy with such strong leadership abilities on the field could also be so soft-spoken in the booth.

Initially, he was so fearful of the microphone and didn't want to come across to viewers as being too overbearing. It was a tough task simply getting him to project his voice in a proper and effective manner. Honestly, it was as tough a job as I've ever had trying to help someone become a lot better than they thought they realized they could be. I'd venture to say that Derrick probably also thought it was one of the hardest things he's ever had to do.

But Derrick did it. He got through it and became a really good color analyst. It showed me how willing he was to learn and how determined he was to pick up on things—even things that didn't come naturally to him.

When I accepted the position of commerce secretary under Governor Ernie Fletcher, I insisted that Derrick become my deputy secretary. Initially they said he was already spoken for, but I wasn't going to have any of that. I brought him on board, and one of the first jobs I tasked him with was to find more qualified African Americans to staff our state parks departments.

Derrick not only brought in Jerry Blanton as the first African American parks commissioner in the history of the state, but he also hired three hundred additional African American workers in a department that previously employed inexcusably few. If you challenged Derrick with a mission, he was going to do it and do it well.

When Derrick first took on the athletics director position at Coppin State, he discussed it with me at length. His basketball coach at the time had been there forever but wasn't getting the job done anymore. Derrick needed to fire him but couldn't pull the trigger.

"Are you the athletics director, or is he?" I asked Derrick. "If you're the athletics director, then you're the one making the decisions."

Derrick ended up making that difficult decision. As he progressed up the leadership ranks, he became all the more decisive, resolute, and purposeful in his decision-making process.

No one with whom I've worked with was more dependable than Derrick. During our 6:30 am staff meetings at Commerce, he was always on time. As a football player, Derrick always bragged about how his teams always scored inside the twenty-yard line. I challenged him to always score inside the twenty in everything he did. Derrick was smart, loyal—and above all else—full of integrity and character.

How Derrick's life has transpired is great reading. He's never been one who's afraid to speak his mind. I love it because of how much he has done and continues to do in giving back to the state of Kentucky and the University.

I am so proud of him, of how he carries himself, and of what he has become. After hearing his story, I'm certain you'll feel the same.

Prologue

I *heard them booing me.*

My senior season in 1977 at the University of Kentucky started out with more of a fizzle than a bang. That summer, I had opened my big mouth when *SEC Magazine* interviewed me as Kentucky's featured starting quarterback. I predicted that we were going to go undefeated. Not only did I say it, but I believed it with every fiber of my being.

Coach Curci, however, didn't take to my bravado too kindly. He called me immediately over to his house and told me in no uncertain terms why I shouldn't have said what I said. He mentioned a few things that I hadn't really thought too much about. On any team, the guys on the offensive line are always the hardest to replace. We had lost three starters from our O-line, including our star offensive tackle Warren Bryant—a guy you simply could not replace.

I understood all of that but thought our defense would be strong enough to carry the team until the offense found its rhythm. As it turned out, it took a bit longer than I imagined for our offense to get untracked.

We barely beat North Carolina 10 – 7 after beating them fairly handily in the Peach Bowl the year before. We pulled the game out at the end when North Carolina's punt returner muffed a punt and gave us great field position for a final scoring drive. It dawned on me afterwards that maybe Coach Curci was right. This was going to be a lot harder than I had ever imagined.

We went down to Baylor next, and Mike Deaton—my backup—was able to put up our only points in a disappointing 21 – 6 defeat. We had poor field position all day, I didn't play very well, and we lost our starting fullback, Rod Stewart, to a season-ending ACL injury. Plus, Baylor had a pretty tough defense led by a guy named Mike Singletary. They gave us more than we could handle that day.

When we arrived back in Lexington, reporters were coming up and asking me about Mike Deaton and whether there was now a quarterback controversy. They hinted that perhaps he was going to replace me the very next week. I couldn't believe what they were saying. I responded emotionally, told them, "Screw you," and just walked away.

Remember, Mike came out of high school as the Kentucky Player of the Year. Everyone wanted him to play well and succeed. In our next game at home against West Virginia, Mike didn't get the start—I did. And our offense finally started to produce like I knew we could. We were ahead by two or three touchdowns when the fans started booing me as I came back on the field for our next series.

WHY WERE THEY BOOING ME? Sure, I was wrong in saying we were going to go undefeated at the beginning of the year. But just because they wanted to see Mike play shouldn't have been a reason to boo me. I came from a place where home fans never booed their own players. I felt that fans in Lexington were turning on me simply because of my skin color. And I was mad.

Billy Reed of the *Louisville Courier Journal* interviewed me after the game. He congratulated me on the win before asking me what I thought about the fans booing me. If we weren't friends, Billy really could have made me look bad because I blurted out some things to him that wouldn't have been well received by the UK faithful.

"Screw these fans," I remember saying to him. "As far as I'm concerned, they can all go to hell. They don't know crap about winning. All I'm playing for is me and the guys who are in this locker room."

What I meant by those comments was that I wasn't afraid of anybody. They could take their boos and shove it. They had no earthly idea what I was all about. Of the fifty-eight thousand people in Commonwealth Stadium that day, I knew there weren't a thousand people in the stands that looked like me.

A couple of my teammates overheard my comments and tried to get me to tell Billy that I didn't really mean what I said. Screw them. My dad always told me not to let others know what I was thinking. At that point, however, I was so mad that I didn't care. My parents sat right behind the bench. They could hear all the hurtful N-words. "Get that [boy] out of there. Put so-and-so in instead." The fans didn't hide any of that garbage. I was sick and tired of it all. All fifty-eight thousand of them could have come on down, and I would have taken them all on.

The next day, the newspaper headlines blared, "Ramsey tells fans to go to hell." It was bad, but not nearly as bad as it could have been. Even with Billy's toned-down narrative, Coach Curci called me that Sunday night and told me I was going to apologize for my remarks. I refused. I told him I wasn't taking anything back.

"Well, Derrick, when the quarterback's playing well, you get all the glory," he said. "You have to understand that when things don't go well, you have to stand up for that part of the job also."

I thought I was doing exactly just that—standing up for me and for all the other people that looked like me. The fans' backlash was not going to get in the way of what I wanted to accomplish. The people that had taught me and invested in me had prepared me for exactly this kind of reception. I was ready. What's more, my whole team supported me throughout the entire ordeal. They knew exactly what I stood for. I wasn't going to apologize for how I felt and what I said.

Or should I?

This was a watershed moment for me. I had to decide whether to stand my ground. Fifty years later—after everything I lived through before and since—I still think I made the right decision.

1

Hastings, Florida

"Your job is to get to the table," my dad said to me one day when I was just six years old. "You either get to the table, or whatever scraps fall off, that's what you're left with. But if you get to the table, then you get to divide stuff up. You get to be part of the decision-making process. You get to decide how much goes to this person or that person."

I never forgot those words. All my life, I've been trying to get to the table. This is my story.

Humble Beginnings

I came calmly into the world on Sunday, December 23, 1956, at five-thirty in the afternoon. There were no blaring trumpets or loud sirens heralding my arrival. In fact, the local doctor delivered me within the nurturing walls of my cozy, twelve hundred square foot childhood home—the fourth of five children born to my hardworking parents, Rudolph and Elizabeth Ramsey.

I have very fond memories of my parents as well as of my hometown of Hastings, Florida. Hastings is located on the northeast side of the state, right outside of St. Augustine. Contrary to what people may think, you couldn't find a single orange grove within the city limits. You could, however, grow more potatoes per capita than anywhere else in America.

Here's what I love so much about Hastings. It's a town that I wish every young person could experience growing up—a tight-knit community where everybody supported everybody. It was very much an academic town, and our parents always expected us to do well in school. Remember, this was a time of pre-integration, so the way we saw things in our community was perhaps a bit different than the way things are now. The standards seemed loftier back then. If we didn't excel in our studies, we knew we had no chance to succeed in life.

Hastings, at the time, was about sixty to seventy percent African American. It was a typical southern town. When you come into a southern town, it's divided by two things normally—either the railroad tracks or a body of water. Blacks would live on one side of the tracks and Whites on the other, or Whites would live on one side of the water and Blacks on the other.

Sure enough, our town had these railroad tracks running right through it. On one side of the tracks, it was all White. On the other side, it was all African American. We did not cross those tracks until 1970—my freshman year in high school, when they integrated the schools. Prior to that, the Whites didn't speak to us, and we didn't speak to them. We didn't think anything of it because being segregated was all we knew at the time.

Awesome Parents

At a very young age, I suspected I had awesome parents. They always talked about this big world out there that we had to see. Our little town was just a small piece of it. It was up to us to figure out where we fit in. All five of us kids and our parents would sit around this table, and my dad would share his expectations with us—where he wanted to see us and how he wanted us to be remembered in this community as people who have accomplished things, not people that have excuses about why we didn't make it. My parents believed in me, and I believed growing up that there was nothing too big to tackle. They prepared me to take on whatever came my way.

"At this table, there'll be lawyers, there'll be doctors, there'll be scientists," my mother would always tell us during conversations around the table.

Remember, I'm six or seven years old and having all these expectations ingrained in my mind. What was even more puzzling was that I never really understood where it all came from. My mom had no experiences with education. On her side of the family, my siblings and I were the first ones who would attend college. For her to have this thing about all the great things we kids were going to accomplish, that just always stuck with me. What did she or my dad know about "getting to the table"?

My mom got pregnant when she was only fifteen and gave birth to my sister when she was sixteen. My mom then married my dad who was only eighteen himself at the time. Fortunately for all five of us kids, their beloved marriage would last an amazing fifty-six years.

My dad worked hard during the early years delivering gas—diesel fuel—to the local farmers in our community. He also held a second job as a security guard at the potato grater. My mother was a chef at the hospital. She would come home every day, scramble together some food for us and then head off to her second job as a short-order cook at a little drug store. I got to see two parents working two jobs for nearly two decades. This whole thing about work ethic I got firsthand from watching my mom and dad on a daily basis. They set a great example right in front of our faces.

Looking back, I was somewhat astonished at the emphasis my parents put on schooling. I'll say it again. For my mom and dad to be able to understand the value of education when they had very little of it themselves growing up was amazing in my mind. I owe everything to my parents—for their vision and for them always challenging us. They constantly made us aware that even though we all played sports—that we were gifted athletes in football, basketball, and track—education was far more important in the long run.

We never lost sight of that. I realized what was important at an early age. Coincidentally, it seemed all my close friends were good students as well. Being a star athlete in our community was something we all took for granted. I got no special treatment for being good at sports. My brothers were All-State players already. My mom was a legendary basketball standout in her own right. My dad had been a star player when he was young. Being a good student was what mattered to him and to the other parents.

Because of that strong focus on academics, we've had a lot of very successful people come out of our little town. One of our neighbors, the Bartleys, lived in a modest house just like ours. They started out like everyone else—working the potato fields. But two of the Bartley brothers went on to become scientists at NASA, as did their uncle. Their youngest brother was on the faculty at the University of Kentucky.

It turned out that in this little community of 650 people, we had lawyers, pharmacists, doctors, and Ph.Ds., all descended from parents who—in most cases—didn't have a high school diploma themselves. That included my mother, who didn't get her high school diploma until after I graduated from UK.

Maybe I shouldn't be so surprised. After all, everyone wants their kids to do a whole lot better in life than they did. In the African American community, that's always been the mindset and the norm. We're always going to be measured by the next generation.

<u>High-Achieving Siblings</u>

As kids, we never wanted to let our parents down. And as it turns out, we didn't. The Ramseys all studied hard, earned a decent living, and became productive citizens later in life.

My oldest sibling, Mildred Joyce Ramsey, was nine years older than I was. She and I ended up being the closest of the clan. She retired after thirty-five years in elementary education.

Next in line was my oldest brother, Rudolph Tyrone Ramsey. He was named after my dad and was born seven years before me. He retired as a principal of the largest high school in St. Augustine.

After him came Robert, who was six years older than me. He retired as a lieutenant colonel in the Air Force before becoming city commissioner of Lexington and then secretary of personnel for the commonwealth of Kentucky. I was deputy secretary of commerce during that same timeframe. It was actually the first time in Kentucky where two brothers served concurrently as secretaries in state government.

Ty and Bob would always beat up on me as kids. They didn't do it in a bad way—it was just what big brothers did to little brothers. Make no mistake, I admired them and always looked up to them. They were both good athletes. My sister and brothers were also excellent students. It was natural for me to try and find my mark whenever we competed against each other.

I remember when my brothers would come home from college, I'd be so excited to see them. I'd be waiting at the door just wanting to go do something with them. It didn't matter what we did—but just to be with my big brothers was the coolest thing for me.

My youngest brother, Reggie—the baby of the family—was born nine years after me. He retired from the Army and then went to work for homeland security and later for the federal government doing intelligence.

Grandparents

As you can see, my parents set a high bar for all their children. Going back a generation, my grandparents most likely did the same with them. Living in the same town, we all spent a lot of time together as a family. It's funny the things you remember about your grandparents. One thing always puzzled me about my maternal grandmother. She acted way more partial to her granddaughters than to her grandsons.

For example, summers in Hastings were so hot. We had only one air conditioning unit in the whole house. My grandmother would allow the girls to come inside to cool off, while the boys had to stay outside. These houses at the time were all built up on bricks, so the boys could crawl under the house where it was a bit cooler. We tried to explain to my grandmother that there were also snakes and spiders and everything else that lurked around underneath there, but she remained unsympathetic.

I remember my paternal grandmother, by contrast, was always more partial to us boys. She always had Jell-O, Nestle Quik, a pie, or a cake ready for us when we dropped in. We only lived about a hundred yards apart, so I went over to her house quite often. I felt a lot more at ease during my visits with her.

Playing Ball

As a young boy, football ultimately captivated me—but basketball fast became my main love because of my mother's legendary status as a basketball player in our hometown. She would often come outside after work and shoot baskets with me and my friends. We were all impressed by the things she could do with a basketball in her hands.

Our town was loaded with local sports legends. When I was nine, I was honored to be the waterboy for our high school football team. My brother was the starting center, and my cousin was the starting guard. Not to mention, we had the most electrifying quarterback ever—a guy named Clewis Wright. Boy, I wanted to be just like him. It seemed like everybody looked up to Clewis and wanted to follow him, but I didn't exactly know why at the time. Watching Clewis was the first time the leadership bug bit me.

I started reading all sorts of books on leadership. One of the first ones I purchased and read cover to cover was *Quarterbacking* by Bart

Starr. It explained to me what professional leadership—and more importantly, what winning—was all about. For your team to win and do well, the leader and quarterback had to play well. I knew right then that I wanted to play quarterback. I wanted to be the leader.

With regard to leadership—especially leading young people—you have to lead with a heavy hand. In other words, if you want your teammates to follow, you have to be unrelenting in your approach. As a young leader, you're always going to be challenged. Your peers will always think they know as much as you. Therefore, to be effective, you have to show them you're in charge.

"Just shut the hell up," I'd frequently say in the huddle. "This is how we're going to do it."

Of course, it helps if you're also talented and have success in what you do. I spent many hours honing my quarterback skills right inside Hastings on our side of the railroad tracks. With all our home-grown talent, we didn't see the need to venture out much at all. The only time my dad left town during those early years was when he took my sister and brothers back to college. I remember going with him once to see a game at Bethune-Cookman, where my sister went to school. The quarterback for the Wildcats also just happened to be from Hastings. It was so neat and exciting to be able to cheer him on.

During this time, one of the most legendary football coaches in the state was Jake Gaither at Florida A&M. He was much like Eddie Robinson at Grambling, John Merritt at Tennessee State, and Marino Casem at Alcorn State. If Jake Gaither wanted you, and you were from the state of Florida, you were going to play for him at Florida A&M. The great Bob Hayes went to Florida A&M. One of my teammates, Henry Lawrence, who was a first-round pick by the Oakland Raiders went there also. I could have easily followed in their footsteps and wound up there myself.

Tyrone Ramsey—*In His Own Words*

"Derrick never got into trouble growing up. In fact, we were all pretty well behaved. Our mom made sure of that. If we ever stepped out of line, we got a beating. And whenever we got a beating, we also got a speech. Even though Derrick was much younger than Bob and me, he still got the same treatment from them. We all learned our lessons quickly.

Derrick was a better quarterback than Clewis Wright. Clewis had a radical arm, but he'd occasionally panic. He'd get nervous standing back there behind the line. Derrick never panicked. He'd just stand there calmly and pick out his receivers.

Derrick always had such an easygoing personality. Back in our hometown of Hastings, everybody knew him and liked him. My brother never met a stranger he wouldn't talk to, and everybody who talked to him remembered his name. His personality and talents have taken him a long way—to a lot of fabulous places that I've never made it to. He's done a lot of things that I wished I could have done. I'm so happy that he got the opportunities to play on the main stage.

I'm very proud of Derrick. He's done a fantastic job with not only his life in sports but also with his personal life. In everything he does, he's always trying to get to the next level. There's nothing he thinks that he can't do. Our parents instilled that type of thinking in all of us from the very beginning. Remember this: in everything you do, you're representing the family.

Even in retirement, Derrick's always thinking two steps ahead about the next project he wants to tackle. He's never going to slow down and just chill. That's where he and I are different. When I retired after thirty-eight years in education, I said, 'I'm done.' That's not going to happen with Derrick."

Al, Frankie, and Joe

Solid friendships have always been important to me. My closest childhood friends were Al, Frankie, and Joe. The four of us were inseparable—young classmates who planned on growing up, going to college together, and eventually winding up on each other's coaching staff as we mapped out our careers in the sporting world.

As kids, we would just do boy stuff—like playing football and basketball in the backyard. There were no blacktop courts in Hastings, so we'd often break into our school gym for a decent court to play on. Whatever we did, we mostly did it together.

Interestingly enough, we all ended up going to different colleges. I went to Kentucky, Al went to Austin Peay, Frankie went to Bethune-Cookman, and Joe went to South Carolina State.

Joe graduated from South Carolina State where he played with the great Harry Carson. They were awesome teammates, and I was extremely proud of Joe when his team won their conference championship. Years later, Joe became a school principal.

Al and I got into a heated dispute once because I wanted him to come to Kentucky to be with me. He went to Austin Peay instead. After his freshman year there, he decided he didn't want to stay in school at all, so he joined the Navy. I felt like Al broke our deal, so I didn't speak to him for several years.

After his stint in the Navy, Al became a prison guard. While working, he decided to go back to college. Al is a smart guy and had so much promise. It turned out that he just sidetracked his education temporarily by going to the military first. He eventually got his degree, and Joe brought him on as his basketball coach at his school. When I became the athletics director at Kentucky State University in 1999, I called Al to see if he wanted to become an assistant coach at the college level. He decided he wanted to remain a high school coach. A couple of years ago, Al recorded his 300th win. I'm extremely proud of him also.

Frankie got his degree in business from Bethune-Cookman, but he never officially applied it toward a future career. All these years, he's been a farmer. And he's made more money than all of us by growing potatoes and cabbages.

Even though the four of us all went our separate ways, it all started with us being little boys trusting each other and dreaming big about what we could all do. As young people, we were all dreamers, and that's why I think we all had success. We bucked the odds.

Frankie grew up in a single-parent home with his mother. Al lived with his aunt. Joe was adopted. I was the only one who had both parents around. But that never got in the way of our friendship, our thoughts, our dreams, or our plans of what we were going to accomplish down the line. The differences in how we were raised at home didn't seem to affect us at all.

My friendships with Frankie, Al, and Joe have meant so much to me. To this day, they're still three of my closest friends. Every time I go home, I see them, and we spend time together. We talk about everything. It just shows you that I didn't get where I got by myself. My friends are a huge part of who I am.

During the time I was working for Governor Ernie Fletcher, George W. Bush was running for president. David Williams, the president of the Senate, asked me to ride with him and Bush to a fundraiser in Louisville. For forty-five minutes, I got to talk with George Bush. He's often misunderstood, but he's such a kind man.

After Bush became president, I told Al, Frankie, and Joe that I got to meet and speak with him. Of course, they didn't believe me.

"Aw Deke, you're lying. You didn't meet no damn president," they said.

I whipped out my cell phone and showed them pictures and video of me having conversations with the President of the United States. Growing up in Hastings, Florida, I never could have imagined that happening in a million years.

Just recently, Al visited me in Lexington. Because I'm on the University of Kentucky Board of Trustees, I get to go to the President's Suite before games. All these senators and congressmen are also in there wanting to come up and talk to me.

"Man, Derrick, I can't believe this," Al whispers to me. "You introduce me to the president, and the president is talking to me. The senators are all talking to me. Everybody wants to talk with you. Can you believe the life you've lived?"

No, I cannot. It turns out that I've met leaders from all over the world—from Tehran to Dubai. Years ago, I met Ronald Reagan. Think about it. I'm a kid with big dreams, but even I couldn't have drawn this up.

The Dream Begins

Many think my path from such humble beginnings in Hastings to cabinet secretary in the highest levels of state government makes for a unique and compelling story. You're probably already wondering how I ended up being so closely aligned with the Republican Party. After all, being Black and a Republican is a difficult path in this day and age.

Although both of my parents were devout Democrats, our values growing up aligned closely with those of the Republican Party. Fiscally, my mom and dad were extremely conservative. They certainly didn't believe in lavish spending, and there's no way they would have ever taken a government subsidy. They were way too proud and would have worked their fingers to the bone to avoid any sort of handout. Moving up in the world as a family meant not accepting any government cheese whatsoever.

The Republican way back then was pulling yourself up by your bootstraps. I saw firsthand how my parents valued hard work. That was how we were going to succeed in this world. It was a concept that was instilled in me early on and also made a lot of sense to me even as a kid.

Congressman Jack Kemp became a big Republican influence on me during my young adult years. Kemp had played quarterback for the Buffalo Bills and was good friends with my Oakland Raider teammate Gene Upshaw. He and I would have a lot of interesting and insightful conversations about "people under the tent." He constantly empha-sized to me how the Republican Party had to be more inclusive. He and Ronald Reagan were also close friends, so I got a heavy dose of what Reagan and the Republican Party stood for. As a young adult carving out a career, I could relate to a lot of their political ideology.

When I became actively involved in state government during the Fletcher administration, it hit me how the Democratic Party had pre-viously misled so many of my fellow African Americans. During that time, Governor Fletcher's Republican administration hired more Afri-can Americans at director-level positions and higher than at any other point in the state's largely Democrat-controlled history. How could that be if the Democrats were supposedly for us? How could that pos-sibly be if the Democratic Party really stood for diversity and equality? The numbers simply didn't add up.

I still get a lot of pushback from African Americans wondering why I'm not affiliated with the Democratic Party. My response is always, "That may work for you, but it doesn't work for me." I'm not saying the Republican Party is perfect. It's just that it aligns a lot more with my core values.

Politics aside, all I wanted as a kid was to be a professional football player. In our county, there had only been one pro before me. People thought I was crazy. I was eight years old running around town with a football under one arm and a bag of groceries under the other. Years later, when I made it to my first Super Bowl, the whole town was in disbelief. When I celebrated my second one, everyone was still incre-dulous.

I guess the dream started fairly early. I knew at a young age that I was good in sports. My dad told me I was going to be good, and I be-lieved everything my dad said. I was also bigger than everybody else. In fourth grade, I was already a head taller than my classmates. I used to slump down because I wanted to fit in with all the other kids.

I liked all sports as a young boy. When you're poor, you just play whatever is in season. You play football during football season. You play basketball during basketball season. You play anywhere you can. Most of the time it's in your backyard. There was no community gym or rec center in Hastings to hang out at. But that didn't matter to us. All we needed was a ball, and somebody always had one.

Day after day, I kept growing bigger and stronger. My mother was very smart. Most kids didn't like vegetables—squash and spinach and greens and carrots. My mother told me that if I was going to be a football star, I had to eat that stuff. She said that's how I'd get my muscles. So, I would eat everything. There was nothing I didn't like, sweets included. Plus, my mother was a great cook, so everything she made was my favorite.

We had potatoes every way imaginable. Because we didn't have much money, we had to make things stretch. My dad only made fifty dollars a week. He'd stick it in an envelope, and that envelope went directly to my mom because she handled all the money. Us kids never knew it at the time, but we were probably one paycheck away from being in trouble. Even in 1999, when my dad retired, his take home pay amounted to only $302 a week.

Dad would deliver gas to farmers, and they would give things to him just because they liked him. Oftentimes they'd give him half a deer or a tub of fish. Mom would then cook it up and stretch those dollars. Because of all the fields around us, we always had as much cabbage, or as many potatoes or greens as we wanted or needed.

On holidays and birthdays, we always got a little something special. It was never very much, but we were always okay with it. I was fine with just having my siblings around and celebrating time together as family.

I learned about the value of money early on. I was nine years old and decided to start my first business doing lawn services for the neighbors. I asked my mom for some money to buy me a lawnmower. With the fifteen dollars I borrowed, I eagerly headed down to the local Western Auto and purchased a cheap lawnmower, a gas can, and some gas.

On my first day out, I made about twenty bucks. I immediately tried to repay my mom the fifteen dollars I borrowed from her earlier. I proudly told her we were even. She quickly took the fifteen dollars and surprised me with what she said next.

"Oh no baby," she answered. "We're not even. We're partners. You wouldn't have ever gotten started without my money. We're fifty-fifty partners."

My mom wasn't going to let me keep any of my hard-earned money. Knowing that I'd spend it on something frivolous, she wisely took that money and bought savings bonds with it. She taught me a valuable lesson early on about putting your money to work for you. I still have those savings bonds today. They're only worth about seven thousand dollars. But the reason I keep them is that they have "Derrick and Elizabeth Ramsey" inscribed on them. Having those memories means the world to me.

At home, there were always chores to do. My mom was a strict disciplinarian. *SHE DID NOT PLAY!* When your feet hit the floor in the morning, you had better have your bed made up. Everything always had to be clean. Everything always had its place. If we messed up, we got a spanking. Actually, I wouldn't call it a spanking. No, no, no…I'd call it a whoopin'.

I got most of my whoopin'(s) when I got sidetracked due to sports. My mom would send me to the store. On the way, I'd see these guys playing football. "Hey Deke," they'd call out. "Come play with us." So, I'd end up playing football rather than going to the store for my mom. Sports sidetracked me every single time.

School Days

School was another matter altogether. In Hastings, from first to twelfth grade, we had 350 total students. My brother and sister had a graduating class of maybe eighteen people. But it's not the quantity of the students but the quality of the education we received that stands out. Yes, the schools were still segregated, but I never had a class with more than twelve to fifteen people. You couldn't hide in a class that size. You had to turn in all your assignments. If you didn't turn in all your assignments, the teachers would call your parents or perhaps stop by your house.

I never had any problems, though. I loved school. I got a lot of pleasure out of it because our teachers made everything a competition. When they taught us how to write cursive, the one who did the best got a prize. There was always competition.

I adored my first-grade teacher, Ms. Hadley. Her husband was the principal. I knew she liked me a lot because she always kept me close to her. She always had her arm around my shoulder. I learned later on that Ms. Hadley held on to a bunch of my first-grade papers long after I left her class. She showed them to my sister during one of her visits back home. These are the types of long-lasting relationships that defined my childhood and that I cherished moving forward into my adult career.

These teachers, as you'll see, genuinely cared about me for whatever reason. It wasn't just a matter of them going through the motions, getting me through for the year, and moving on to the next class. There was something more to it. I was always respectful to them and always tried to do what I was supposed to do. I don't know why they singled me out. Perhaps they just thought I was someone who was slow who needed extra attention. Either way, I'm very thankful for their influence. I hope I made them all proud.

My third-grade teacher, Ms. Humphrey, was my cousin. She was very demanding. She didn't favor anybody. You did things her way and that was it. I respected teachers like that and would later mimic that leadership style during my days in athletics administration and government.

Ms. Carter, my fourth-grade teacher, was my friend Al's aunt. She was this African American woman who stood about five-foot-seven. She was beautiful, but she was a BIG woman. She probably weighed 250 pounds. Ms. Carter was also no nonsense and pushed us all the time to be the best. She gave me such a sense of pride.

"Derrick, stand up," she'd say to me. "Roar out with that big deep voice of yours. Rare those shoulders back."

There was always competition in Ms. Carter's class. We'd be working on addition. She'd bring two of us to the front of the room and give us math problems to work out. Whoever figured out the problems first would be the winner. We'd have spelling bees where everybody had to stand up. When you couldn't spell a word, you had to sit down. The last one standing would be the winner. It was in Ms. Carter's class that I discovered how much I loved winning.

In school, math was my favorite subject. It always was and always has been my best subject. I didn't like studying subjects like history or civics at all. My sixth-grade teacher, Mr. Campbell, said to me once, "One day, people will be reading about YOU. Isn't it cool to know who came before you?" That got me interested in history.

I was also interested in girls. I had my eye on a lot of them early on. The girls in my class were all beautiful girls. However, I didn't want to become friends with them because once you got close to them, you had to think about asking them out if you liked them. It was awkward. Plus, my parents kept me focused on what was important. I didn't want girls to get between me and my dreams of winning.

That love of winning translated quickly from the classroom to the athletic courts. As fourth graders, Frankie, Al, Joe, and I would beat the fifth and sixth-grade intramural teams on a consistent basis. Our team—the Jaguars—won the intramural championships three years in a row. During that time, I had figured out that if they kept score, then I wanted to win. It didn't matter if I was making baskets, scoring touchdowns, or shooting marbles, *I WANTED TO WIN!*

I started playing on the school football and basketball teams in the spring of my sixth-grade year. At the time, there were no freshman or JV teams. There was only one team for the whole school. It consisted of about twenty-seven of us, and we all traveled around on the same bus. Joe and I started out as practice dummies for the first three years. Finally, we broke through as freshmen. Joe became the starting linebacker, while I was the alternating starting quarterback.

Our teams were always good. I don't think my brothers were ever on a team that lost more than one game. I wasn't there of course when my dad played, but everyone in the community talked about how good he was. They always referred to me as one of Rudy's boys. Everybody expected Rudy's boys to win and succeed.

Robert Ramsey—*In His Own Words*

"Our family had a great relationship growing up. I would think we're some of the closest siblings you're ever going to run across. Sadly, we've lost our older sister and youngest brother already. That hurts us a little bit, but that's part of life. We were such a close-knit family, including our grandmothers, and aunties, and such. All those folks did their best to protect us.

The Ramsey household was a disciplined household—especially from our mother's side. She expected all of us to work hard. That meant getting up and getting a job during the summer months when school was out. None of us were bad kids growing up. We didn't get into a whole lot of trouble. We tried our best to conform to the norms that the household had established.

I remember all of us boys slept in the same room. Our oldest brother, Tyrone, and I were bunkmates. In our part of Florida, it got pretty cold in the wintertime. It was nice having somebody else there to keep your bed warm. Derrick was several years younger than us, so he usually slept in his own bunk.

All of us played ball. Ty—for his size—was one of the best centers you'd ever run across. I was a band member until my junior year in high school. I made the team and started right away, but there was really no obvious push for any of us. We just all assumed that we'd somehow play sports.

Coach Andy Hinson was a guy we all looked up to. In fact, I pledged his fraternity when I got to college. He was always concerned about the upbringing of the young men and women within the community. He's a great guy, and we all love him to death. He was also a strict disciplinarian. If you didn't do what you were supposed to do, you took it in the shorts.

My parents really valued education. Both of them could have gone to college. Since they didn't, they wanted to make sure all of us had every opportunity available to get our degrees. *From day one, we all knew we were headed for universities. That mindset wears on you and eventually becomes part of your own makeup. Having all of their children graduate from college made our parents very proud, I'm sure.*

As his big brother, I'm very proud of everything Derrick has accomplished. We always knew he had the potential. He just kept on moving forward and up. I call him a proud citizen who's making wherever he goes a little better than what it was when he found it. Derrick's also very focused. He's very much into people and seeing everyone around him excel whenever possible. Whenever he has an opportunity to help someone, he's the first one out of the gate.

I'm not a title kind of guy, but being Kentucky state secretaries at the same time with Derrick was great. When you take care of the tasks at hand, opportunities present themselves. Hard work and dedication landed us both in spots like that at the same moment.

So much of who Derrick is—and who we all are—comes back to what our parents instilled in us. It also comes down to the relationships you've developed with people across the years. You always want to remember where you came from and all the people who helped you along the way. You'll soon discover that Derrick's exactly that kind of guy."

Al Carter—*In His Own Words*

"Whenever you hear of a community raising kids together, Hastings, Florida, was that community. Derrick and I and our friends were under the thumb of everyone in that community. I got spankings from people in that community other than my parents. If I did something wrong with Derrick at his house, we'd both get a whoopin' by his mom. I'm going to tell you the truth—I was afraid of her. She'd beat your behind.

The community held us accountable everywhere we went. I think that's why we all turned out to be pretty decent human beings. Everyone wanted us kids to stay out of trouble, get a good education, and maximize our potential—to either be good athletes, or good in academics—to find something that would lead to a good future. As a result, many people from our little town went on to have outstanding professional careers.

I met Derrick in kindergarten. Our fathers were friends, and I guess it just trickled down to us. Mr. Rudy was a big influence on me. He called me his son also.

Derrick, Frankie, Joe, and I were all athletic guys. We all knew football and sports. Sports was something that tied our community together. It was something we were proud of. Derrick and I walked around all the time talking about how we were going to be professional athletes. Well, Derrick was the only one who turned out to be the professional athlete, and we're all so very proud of that. The rest of us, however, didn't quite maximize our athletic opportunities.

We were also all very competitive in the classroom—always trying to beat each other by getting better grades. But our families were so close that we just looked out for each other all the time. We never pulled each other down due to the closeness of our friendship. It was enjoyable seeing our friends succeed.

Here's how close Derrick and I became. We have nearly identical social security numbers. I remember us walking to the post office together to collect our numbers. After we walked out, we noticed that his social was only one digit lower than what mine was.

For the most part, Derrick was very well behaved while we were growing up. His parents made sure of that. He pretty much stayed out of trouble. But just like all the other teenage boys at that time, Derrick really liked girls. That's all I got to say about that.

Even though Derrick was a star athlete, he would always take time out with the younger kids to encourage them. He was very comfortable speaking with everyone. When we had to make speeches in high school, Derrick pulled it off with ease. You saw back then that he was going to be a great leader.

I never saw Derrick becoming involved politically like he is now. As kids, I don't ever remember us even discussing politics. Being thrust into the environment like he was in the '70s was probably the catalyst that got him started down that path.

Derrick always had a good heart. He was always empathetic and tried to help people whenever he could. What he's done for the state of Kentucky should show everyone how committed he is to the education of our young people. The more opportunities we present to our youth, the sharper they can become and the more they'll stay out of trouble. Idle time is the devil's workshop.

Derrick is an inspiration to me. That's my homeboy. We come from similar roots, and even though we're both on the other side of the mountain now, we're still trying to help people out. I hope we both keep moving in that direction."

Pleasing Dad

My mom and dad came to watch all my games. They usually remained fairly calm and tried to blend in. As long as he was happy with the way I was playing, my dad didn't interfere or try to coach me in any way.

In my sophomore year, we had this big tackle that a lot of schools were looking at. On this particular night, the University of Kansas was there to recruit him. Our stadium only held about seven or eight hundred people, so everyone was bunched in real closely. I could hear my dad yelling, "Derrick. Derrick. Son, you gotta get the lead out. What are you doing? We've got these scouts out here, and you're just here going through the motions. You gotta pick it up."

I did pick it up because I always listened to my dad. I always knew when he was disappointed in me, and I never wanted to let him down. Throughout my life playing football, I put a lot of pressure on myself to succeed because I knew my dad lived through me. He knew I had all this ability, and he didn't want me to waste any of it. He wanted other people to see how good I was also.

Every Sunday, my dad would watch pro football together with a group of other men. The women always cooked for the men at these gatherings. When I was nine or ten, my dad started taking me to these get togethers. After taking time to explain parts of the game to me, he'd point to me and say to all his friends, "This is going to be my pro right here." It made me feel so good that my dad felt so strongly about me in front of his friends.

My dad believed in discipline also. He always told me that lack of discipline will get you beat every time. It didn't matter if you were Black, White, or whatever, if you got out of place, he would let you know. Later on in life, my coaches would tell me the same thing. My dad was always one step ahead of everybody. He was so smart and talented that he could have easily gone on to play college football had family life not intervened.

Until my dad passed, he was my concierge. Any decisions that I made regarding my career, he'd be the guy I would talk to. He had this innate ability to see things and reason things out. He just seemed to always know who was looking out for their own best interest instead of my best interest. He'd always preface his advice to me by saying, "Son, I'm not trying to tell you what to do. But if I were you, this is what I would do." He was always right.

Working for Wealth

My dad worked so hard. I didn't get to see too much affection from my parents because they were too busy working. That's all they did. I didn't really see how their marriage worked either. Partly because of that, marriage was never in the equation early on for me. I had to acquire wealth first. When you came from where I came from—where you got one car, one little house, a bunk bed where you and your brothers all slept together on—you had to have wealthy dreams. If you didn't see it, how could you believe that you can be it?

Once I had seen what wealth was about, I wanted it. And the only way to get it was to work for it. I worked mowing lawns as a kid, worked through the summers in college, and worked every offseason when I played professional football. I didn't just sit back and fat cat when I started making a salary. No, I managed it and took some risks with it along the way. It saddens me when I see athletes today just totally squander all the money they worked so hard to make.

Once again, I just give so much thanks to my parents for preparing me and protecting me financially. Although we didn't have much growing up, we made the most with what we had. In fact, most of our neighbors thought we had a lot more than we actually did. We didn't have any more than anybody else. My parents just knew how to manage what they had better than anybody else. They passed a lot of those valuable lessons on to us.

Each year, I'd get a pair of hushpuppies, a pair of hard shoes, two or three pairs of jeans, one pair of slacks, and a couple of shirts. That would be my wardrobe allowance for the year. It was certainly adequate, but it wasn't like I was walking around with a nice pair of Cole Haans on my feet.

Actually, all the cool athletes were wearing Chuck Taylor All Stars during that time. I was still wearing those no name Pro Stars. My mom told me that if I continued to excel at football and basketball, I wouldn't have to worry about *buying* the good shoes.

"One day, they're going to pay you to wear these shoes," she said.

My mom was ahead of her time also. When I got to the NFL, they paid me to wear those shoes. Again, where did that foresight come from?

Camps

I first realized I had a chance to attend college on an athletic scholarship when I went to a basketball camp at the University of Jacksonville in 1970. This was when Artis Gilmore was the big center on their team that lost to UCLA in the NCAA championship game.

I was a freshman in high school at the time. I worked my tail off to earn the ninety dollars it cost to attend that week-long camp. There were 500 kids at that camp, and I was one of the best ones there. The best player was a senior named Johnny Alberry. I'll never forget it. He could jump like nobody's business.

The camp opened my eyes to how good I could be. I received the defensive player of the camp award. Although I was playing against seniors, they weren't much bigger than me. As a freshman, I was already six-foot-two, and I was playing to win. And I was also playing for my future. When my parents dropped me off, they would always remind me, "Remember why you came here. This isn't a vacation. You came here to handle your business."

Handling my business meant getting recognized. My parents were fully supportive of my athletic accomplishments, but never at the expense of my schoolwork. They saw too many guys who were really good on the field but didn't have any grades. Those guys went nowhere. My parents weren't going to let me fall into that trap.

In my freshman and sophomore years, I had the privilege of playing with the greatest basketball player ever from Hastings—Fred Cave. We called him "Thirsty." Fred was a senior that year and could shoot like nobody's business. He should have had a fabulous college career—as the starting two-guard opposite John Lucas at Maryland—but his grades let him down. That wasn't going to happen to me.

There are so many factors that go into becoming a true professional. In regard to athletic ability, knowledge of the game, and outright skill, Fred was a pro. He was on a completely different level than the rest of us. It wasn't like he was that much faster or could jump higher than everyone. He just had natural basketball instincts that were off the charts. Always upbeat and smiling, he knew how to play the game.

Sadly, I attended Fred's funeral in 2023. I heard him say once that when I left Hastings after my sophomore year, the entire town just died. Now he's gone also. Rest in peace, my friend.

Other than my basketball camps, our family would seldom travel too far from Hastings. During the summer, my parents would occasionally go to this place called Camp Hillcroft. It's still in existence today. I remember my mom and dad would take time off from their jobs to go cook for these kids at the camp. Me and my two older brothers also served as counselors during a summer or two.

Once a year, we'd also take a family trip to the beach. It was only eighteen miles away, but it was still a big deal. Our church would occasionally have a beach trip or a lake trip also, but that was it as far as vacation trips were concerned for the Ramsey family.

Faith and Church

I've always known that there's a higher being. The things I've been able to accomplish were solely because of God. I had a lot of athletic ability, but all of it was God-given. From a very early age, I understood that for me to be successful, I always had to shine a light on God because that's where it all started, and that's where it's all going to end.

Faith was an important part of life in Hastings. Everybody at that time went to church. In small towns, there seemed like there were more churches than people—with a church on every street corner. As a family, we attended Mount Zion AME Church. Reverend William Desue was our pastor for the biggest part of my childhood. In our community, faith and church were what got us through daily life.

I remember there was this disabled veteran from the next town over who used to come around on Sundays right when church was letting out. He'd ring his bell and sell peanuts to the kids. I'd take the fifty cents my parents gave me to put in the church offering and go buy peanuts with part of the money. My grandmother—the one who I didn't get along with because she liked the girls better—she'd tell my mom on me. She was a *MEAN* lady!

As a family, we all believed that if you were going to be successful, it all begins and ends with God. He deserves the glory. That's not something I've ever been shy about proclaiming. It's not like I flaunted it like a badge of honor, but I didn't wear it under my shirt either.

During the time I played ball, one's personal faith was a lot more private. Nowadays, a lot of kids are just making their faith known for promotional purposes. If professional players are doing it, it's just a matter of time before you see high school players doing it.

I always prayed openly—took a knee in front of my locker before I went out on the field. In high school and college, we prayed as a team. In the NFL, it became much more individualized. I had teammates that weren't believers, but that never bothered me. I believe that your relationship with God is personal, but it's not necessarily private either. I shared my faith with other teammates and participated in prayer groups whenever I could. But I was never overbearing. That wasn't my job. I could introduce them to the Lord, but it was up to them to take it from there.

My parents had a rule that up until you were seventeen, you had to go to church every Sunday. After that, you made your own decisions. That was interesting because my sister graduated high school at sixteen.

My oldest brother graduated at fifteen. I was seventeen when I graduated. By that time, we figured this was just what people do and who they are—they go to church. I didn't mind. I rather enjoyed it.

The longest time I ever went without going to church in my lifetime was during the Covid-19 pandemic. And that was only due to the fact that I had preexisting conditions. I'm a bit embarrassed that I haven't returned regularly since then, but I still read my Bible. I haven't quit praying. All those sermons and Sunday school lessons I got early on at Mount Zion are still with me to this day. My faith has never wavered. I'm trying to grow closer to God every day.

Integration

By 1970, the first year of integration, everyone was a little nervous about the so-called experiment. This was my freshman year in high school, and there were a lot of anxious people watching in our community to see what would happen. Despite the tension, our football team did great. I was the alternating starting quarterback on the team that won the state championship.

In sports, it doesn't matter if you're tall, short, White, Black, or Asian, once you get in that huddle, everyone wants to win. Something about winning heals all. The White school that joined us never won in football while our high school, Harris High, won all the time. It was fun being able to win together, and the entire town was proud of the team. Everyone came to the games and celebrated the victories together. We had never experienced that type of unity in Hastings before.

Playing football eased the tensions in the community, especially regarding how we viewed the world. Remember, until then I had never had a White teacher. Before 1970, all the teachers, principals, counselors, and janitors at our school were African American.

I'd never really thought much about integration before it happened. Suddenly, about two or three weeks before the end of our eighth-grade year, the principal called us into the auditorium and told us that we'd be integrating the schools the very next year. I will never forget his speech.

"This is the day we've been waiting for," the principal said. "Now we get an opportunity to demonstrate that we're smarter than they are, we're better athletes than they are, we're better than they are in everything. That's what we're going to demonstrate when we merge."

I'd always thought of White people as being different. As a young child, I was too young to really grasp the concept, but I'd occasionally hear my parents talk about what was happening in local politics. The first time they mentioned the word "gerrymandering," it really stuck with me.

Our community was mostly African American. But we'd never had an African American mayor. We never had a city council. It was all due to gerrymandering. The district lines for voting in the community were all drawn in such an intentional fashion that African Americans never got to run for public office. White people got to make all the important decisions. I didn't like the fact that they made decisions for ME. They were not only at the table, they WERE the table—and we weren't invited at all. Not only did we not get the scraps, but we weren't getting anything.

The police at that time were all White. As a young kid, my parents warned me to stay in my place. Your place was not to be running your mouth, not to be talking back to the police, or to be talking back to White people, period. Every African American kid at that time was warned that if a White woman is walking on the sidewalk, then get off the sidewalk so that you don't accidently bump into her and cause trouble.

Prior to integration, I rarely encountered any White people. I certainly didn't have any White friends. After integration, all that began to change. I became good friends with my starting center, Wesley Smith. Smitty's mother headed up the kitchen as the main chef in the high school. I'd always get a bigger portion than normal because she had taken a liking to me. I remember going to Smitty's house and teasing his mom.

"This is probably the first time you've had a Black person in your house who wasn't working, huh?" I jokingly said to her.

She laughed and took it all in stride. Her son and I developed this awesome relationship over time. It's amazing the friends you can make when you finally have a chance to spend time with someone. You can't really like someone until you get to know them.

Heroes, Legends, and Black Quarterbacks

When I looked at the White teams playing against us, they were all losing at the time. I didn't want to be a part of that. I was an African American quarterback with dreams of making it big. Even as a high-schooler, I sensed there were barriers. I always looked up, and when you looked up to the NFL, you didn't see any Black quarterbacks.

Every week, *Jet Magazine* spotlighted an African American quarterback on the cover. Each issue cost me twenty-five cents. I would sell soda bottles for money to buy my *Jet*. As a boy, I'd picture myself on the cover.

Eldridge Dickey was on the cover of one of those issues. He was the guy who was going to lead us to the National Football League—the guy who kicked the door open. He ended up being the number one pick by the Oakland Raiders in 1968, and thus became the first African American quarterback selected in the first round of the NFL draft. They called Dickey "The Lord's Prayer" because he was something to behold.

The Raiders also drafted Ken Stabler that same year. When Dickey beat Stabler out as the backup, Stabler left the team and went back home. But the Raiders decided to bring him back and moved Dickey to wide receiver to make room. And thus, Dickey never got to play quarterback. He died in 2000 at age fifty-four, and an article I read said he died of a broken heart. He never got to fulfill his dream as an NFL quarterback.

As a quarterback, when you're at the top of your game, you see things totally different than anyone else on that football field. You are locked in. If you're not two or three plays ahead of the defense, you're going to lose. You gotta be ahead of everyone else. You have to see everything. Not only do you have to know your playbook backwards and forwards, but you also have to learn everybody else's playbook. As a quarterback, I knew what everybody did on every single play. When the Raiders moved me to wide receiver and then tight end, I easily learned those playbooks in a day.

I'm telling you right now that I was smart enough to play any position in the NFL, *including quarterback*. That's not true of everyone. It has nothing to do with what color your skin is. It depends on how smart you are. Unfortunately, there have always been token positions in the league that were based on skin color. Shortly after I entered professional football, there still wasn't a single African American center. They were all White. The inside linebacker position was also all White. Together with free safety, those were all positions for White guys.

Of the four linebackers, the inside linebacker position was the least athletic. That guy could get away with not being able to run. But he was supposedly "smart," so he could make the coverages. If you're a rangy free safety, you don't have to be that athletic, either. They ended up being mostly White guys. As were all the quarterbacks.

To this day, it still bothers me that I didn't get a chance to play quarterback in the NFL. I have no problem if you can beat me out. But it's easy for you to beat me out when I don't get a damn shot at you.

Someone who could have been a great football coach if he only had been given a chance was Nolan Richardson, the 1994 NCAA Championship men's basketball coach at the University of Arkansas. I met Nolan in an elevator at the SEC tournament during the '90s. He was the architect of that frenetic "40 minutes of hell" style of play his teams were known for. He and Rick Pitino had some classic battles.

"I remember you," Nolan said, after I introduced myself and told him how much I enjoyed his coaching style. "I remember you tried to play basketball. But you were much better in football."

Nolan was a football player. He became a basketball coach simply because he knew he'd never get an opportunity to be a head football coach due to him being African American. That was reality back then, and it's still reality today. There are a lot of Black head coaches and general managers in the NBA. You don't see that in the NFL. Nolan was right. Forty years later, not much has changed.

My all-time favorite hero would have to be Jackie Robinson. Not just because of breaking the color barrier in Major League Baseball, but because of his stance in life. It was great what he did on the field, but he was right there with Dr. Martin Luther King Jr. when it came to promoting racial equality.

Muhammad Ali was someone else I admired greatly. He, together with Jim Brown, Bill Russell, Kareem Abdul-Jabbar, and Sam Cooke weren't just great talents, but they were people in our community who spoke out about rights for people of color. It wasn't just their athletic ability and musical talents but their stance and activism within the African American community that made them heroes to me.

As I got older, I wanted to meet Colin Powell in the worst way. I admired and revered him, not only as a general but as an African American man of character. I also admired his political stance as a Republican who voted on issues rather than partisanship. He supported Barack Obama, not because he was an African American, but because he thought Obama was the best candidate for the job. The one time when Colin Powell came to speak at the University of Kentucky, I had to go out of town and missed the opportunity to hear him. I will always regret not getting a chance to shake his hand.

Vernon Jordan, the former civil rights advocate and Bill Clinton advisor, was another figure I admired greatly. You talk about a power broker—this guy was it. In his book, *Vernon Can Read!*, Jordan talks about how—as a young child—he accompanied his mother as she cleaned the house for a wealthy White family. Rather than just watching his mom work, Vernon would go into their library and read everything he could get his hands on. That same family subsequently sponsored him to go to DePauw and Howard University where he then went on to become one of the most powerful political figures in Washington. I was always amazed at his story and how he—as an African American—was able to gather all that influence and power.

As time went on, I became more and more curious about that power. How does someone find that power? Who has the power? How do you use, leverage, and negotiate with the power you have? I would need answers to all those questions as my life played out after my football career.

<u>Winning</u>

But first things first. I talked earlier about my incessant desire to win. All talented athletes want to win, and I've played with a lot of guys who had tons of ability. But everyone has a breaking point. How successful you are depends on your breaking point. How much are you willing to play through? I was willing to play through a lot. As you're going to see, that also took me a long way toward my eventual success.

When you get to the NFL or NBA, everyone there has talent. Everybody on most teams can be a superstar if they gear the offense or defense to showcase their skills. I was first alternate to the Pro Bowl on two occasions. I finished behind Kellen Winslow and Ozzie Newsome. Both of them were in a system where they could catch ninety balls. I was never in that kind of system with the Raiders. My yards per catch were comparable—if not higher—than anybody else's. Everyone knew how good I was. I got to go to Super Bowls. Winslow and Newsome never did.

At the time, those Super Bowl rings meant everything. As a football player, the Super Bowl is the ultimate goal and accomplishment. It's the top of the profession—the standard by which we're measured. I've worn that Super Bowl ring maybe five times.

I've never worn my AFC championship ring. My dad once told me that second place means you're the first loser. For me, football was all about winning and coming in first.

I was in the UK football office recently over at the Nutter Center. This guy was showing some visitors through. On one wall, they had posters of two of Kentucky's great passers—Tim Couch and Jared Lorenzen, who had thrown for a combined 18,769 yards during their college careers.

"Derrick, where are you?" he called out to me, trying to be a little smart mouth. "Where are you on this wall?"

I'm not on the wall, so I told everyone to walk down another hallway with me.

"See that Peach Bowl trophy," I said to them. "See this one that says No. 6 in the country. Those guys you were pointing to? I won more games than both of them combined. Do I want to be on the statistical board? Or do I want to be on the winning board? I prefer to win."

Don't get me wrong. I have a lot of respect for my fellow UK quarterbacks. Take Tim Couch for example. He was the best high school quarterback I'd ever seen. This kid had a touch and understood great placement of the ball. Hall Mumme was the perfect coach for him. But Tim also came with a lot of natural ability. I've never seen a quarterback that young with that kind of ability. And he would listen, too. Some guys think they have all the answers already. He wasn't one of those kids. A dose of humility and a willingness to listen goes a long way to success.

2

Camden, New Jersey

During my freshman year, my high school coach—Andy Hinson—called me into his office to watch some film. By this time, he was already grooming me to be "the guy," and he wanted me to see what a big-time quarterback looked like. We turned on the sixteen-millimeter projector and watched this quarterback roll out to the right and throw a ten to fifteen yard out. He then rolls out to the left and does the same thing with his left hand. Coach Hinson turns the film off and tells me, "You got some work to do."

Coach Hinson always wanted you working and thinking. He never wanted you to believe you were that good already because he always wanted you to figure out how you could get better. He encouraged me plenty but didn't want me to get too big of a head. Unlike some of my other coaches, I had to work hard for his approval. There were a lot of good players from our area. Coach Hinson had no tolerance for knuckleheads.

After my sophomore year, Coach Hinson suddenly told me he'd gotten this new job back in his hometown of Camden, New Jersey. Coach Hinson—who also served as the choir director at our church—would later go on to become the head coach at Bethune-Cookman and Cheney University. But during this time, I just knew him as my football coach. He wanted me to go with him to Camden and be his quarterback.

I didn't know anything about Camden. I didn't know where it was. I was in my own little world in Florida. But Coach Hinson told me that if I went with him and had success, I'd then be able to attend any university in the country. Keep in mind that we had just come off of two state championships at Hastings together. We had won in both my freshman year and my sophomore year.

Before we integrated, our school was known as the Harris High Panthers. After integration, we became the Wildcats. On both of those teams, Coach Hinson ran his offense with alternating quarterbacks. That was how he got the plays in on the field. I accumulated some good stats so that people began to take notice of who I was, but the system we ran didn't really allow for any eye-popping numbers. Our running backs were the ones racking up the yards.

In addition to my prowess on the gridiron, basketball was going well for me also. As a sophomore, I averaged over 15 points a game. People started noticing me on the court, too.

Going to Camden, however, would be a huge change for me. The population of Hastings, Florida, was only 650. My graduating class at Camden High totaled 764. Camden High School had nearly 4500 students altogether. It was a big decision but going there meant national exposure and the opportunity to play against supposedly the best.

Convincing my Mom

"Talk to your parents about it," Coach Hinson said to me. "Let me know what they say."

"Absolutely not," my mom answered. "No way. Don't even think about going there."

My dad, however, was on board. He believed in Coach Hinson because my older brothers had played for him, and he had already been in our community for probably fifteen years or so. The guy had an awesome reputation. Everybody loved and respected Coach Hinson, and he had already sent a number of guys on to small colleges.

I begged my dad to convince my mom to let me go. I reminded him of what Coach Hinson had told me—that if I made the move, I could go to any college I wanted. My parents had always told me to dream big, and now I had this fantastic opportunity to do so.

My dad talked to my mom, but she refused to give in. She would always talk loud enough so that I could hear exactly what she was saying in the next room.

"I haven't finished raising this boy," she'd say to my dad. "He's only fifteen years old. He'll get up there and get in trouble. No way, no how. The answer's 'No!'"

The next morning, I got up at 4:45 to warm the car up for my mom before she left for work. I pleaded with her again. I reminded her that I'd always wanted to be a pro, and this was the best way for me to become one. She just got in her car and drove on to work.

I kept pressuring my dad. I told him we had to do this. He had to believe that I could do this. I hadn't seen the Camden team play, but I just knew I'd be one of the better players when I got up there.

As a last resort, I asked my mom if I could at least go up to Camden for a visit to personally see what it was like. She finally relented.

"Yeah, you can go," she said reluctantly. "But don't get any ideas in your head."

I went up there and I saw this huge school. Wow! They had more students than my sister's college—Bethune-Cookman. They had more students than my brother's college—Florida Memorial. They were almost as big as Florida A&M at that time. I was wide-eyed my whole time there, taken aback by all these huge buildings. Our whole little school in Hastings could have fitted into the Camden cafeteria.

When I returned, my dad said to my mom, "Liz, I've made a decision. The boy's going. Nothing else to talk about."

My mom started crying immediately. My dad pulled me into the back room.

"Let me tell you something, boy," he said. "Nobody makes my wife cry. Nobody—including you. You better make this damn thing work."

Making it Work

I had no doubts I could make this work. I knew where I was as a player—head and shoulders above the average guy in Florida. Although those guys were good, I was still one of the biggest guys out there. I was the quarterback, and I could outrun ninety percent of the people on the field.

Sure enough, when I got to Camden, it felt easy. The competition in Florida had been far superior. Everybody in Florida could run. We only had a few guys in Camden who could really run. My Camden teammates knew I was good also. Before I arrived, there were two guys fighting it out for the starting quarterback position. When I got there, the discussion was over. I recognized early on that I was better than they were and tougher than they were. I saw things differently than everybody else.

Camden High was basically—much like the University of Kentucky—a basketball school. My high school basketball coach put about eight or nine guys in the NBA. They still have a great basketball reputation to this day. D.J. Wagner and Aaron Bradshaw—two recent Kentucky recruits—played there.

Of the 4500 students at Camden, 700 were Puerto Rican, two or three were White kids, and the rest were African Americans. For all intents and purposes, the makeup was very similar to what I had grown up with in a segregated school system. There were, however, a lot of White teachers. That part was very different, but the decision-making administrators were all African American.

I adored my principal, Ms. Cream. She loved athletics, but she loved doing what was right and doing what you were supposed to be doing more than anything. They called our school "Castle on the Hill." You had to walk up a bunch of steps to enter the school. One morning, Ms. Cream caught me coming up the steps rather late. She confronted me about it.

"This isn't going to happen again, is it?" she said to me. "I'm going to give you a pass this time. You know I love you, but I'll be out here from time to time. This better not happen again."

It never did. I knew how she felt about me and how much she expected out of me. I just couldn't let Ms. Cream down.

I'm sure you've heard of her husband. You just don't remember his real name. Do you know who Arnold Cream was? That's Jersey Joe Wolcott, the famous heavyweight boxing champion. Believe it or not, my uncle—Elmer Ray—actually fought against Jersey Joe Wolcott for the heavyweight championship. He lost that fight but came back to beat Jersey Joe in a rematch.

Before I fell in love with football, I wanted to be a boxer because of my uncle. My uncle lived in Los Angeles, and when he came home, he had this special Cadillac. The car was long—it seemed like it went on forever. In our hometown, there were many dirt roads. My uncle would drive on these dirt roads and us kids would just hold on to the back of his Cadillac as if he were returning for a hero's welcome.

Even before training camp started, I got into about four or five fights. This big lineman who played the year before tried to stir things up because his buddy was supposed to be the starting quarterback. He was asking for trouble because when I was growing up, I never saw a fight I didn't like. I whipped his butt in short form. There were two or three other fights that I simply had to dust some other guys off in order to show them that I meant business. I was making a statement early on. I never started a fight. But if you started it, I wasn't going to let you back down.

Coach Hinson took our entire football team to the Pocono Mountains to train that first year. People saw that I was tough, but once they saw what I could do on the football field, their respect for me ratcheted up tenfold.

We called Camden "The High." Our saying at the time was, "You want The High, you got The High." In other words, if you want to challenge us, then bring it. To go to a place like Camden with all this tradition in basketball and being a part of turning the whole city into outright believers in our football team—that was a lofty challenge.

Tough Times at "The High"

Sadly, we only went 2 – 8 that first year. It was the most awful feeling. It hurt. It was insulting, and I was mad all the time. In Florida, our teams won all the time no matter who was playing. This was different. Our team had the ability. They just didn't know how to apply it. Coach Hinson was more than demanding. He was relentless when it came to putting forth effort. He had a way of getting the best out of me using as few words as possible.

When we were practicing in Florida, we didn't get a water break until practice was over. It was ninety-five degrees, and you had to earn your water. Even if you cramped up, too bad. You'll figure it out. When we finally understood what Coach Hinson wanted and what it took to get there, then things started to change.

The guy just loved winning. Winning wasn't accidental for Coach. It didn't involve luck. To him and me both, winning was a combination of hard work, commitment, attitude, and desire.

Hell, everybody wanted to win. But who's willing to get up at five o'clock in the morning and go run? Is everybody willing to run at three o'clock in the afternoon under the blazing hot sun? Not everyone was that committed. I was, and so was Coach Hinson. It was all about winning for us.

I wasn't just the team quarterback, either. I was sort of a player-coach because I knew Coach Hinson's system already. Losing that first year like we did made me even more desiring of learning how to lead and how to get people to follow. I wanted to find out what people were willing to sacrifice in order to achieve our team goals.

Through all of this, most of my regular classmates still really didn't know who I was. I was walking down the hallway one day and I heard a couple of kids talking.

"Man, we brought this big old quarterback up here and we're still sorry as hell," they said.

I just kind of chuckled under my breath and went on about my business. I had no doubts I would eventually succeed. Before I left Hastings, my dad had said I better "make it work." I had no choice. Ultimately my dad had to answer to my mother. He would move mountains to make sure my mother was happy. I had to make it work.

Here was my chance to be like Clewis Wright—our star quarterback back in Hastings. The guy was like Fran Tarkenton. He was phenomenal. He was the show. I used to picture in my mind what he did because that's what I thought a great quarterback should look like. Clewis ultimately won. That's what I was going to do also.

The Turnaround Begins

One day, I walked in the gym and saw it was packed with over three hundred kids. They're there for—of all things—basketball tryouts. You gotta be kidding me. Back in Hastings, we had trouble finding nine guys to play on the team. Now, you have three hundred here trying out for one or two positions. Really?

There was no doubt in my mind I was taking one of those positions. I wasn't trying out. I was sure I was going to be playing—and I was right.

We started our season right after football was over. I ended up being a starter on a team that beat some really good junior college level type teams. We only lost three or four games that whole year. We couldn't play in the tournament that year because the year before, Camden players had gotten into a fight with players from Bishop Eustace—one of the private schools over in Cherry Hill. We had to sit out as part of the penalty, so my junior season in basketball ended a bit prematurely.

The next year in football, our team made an amazing turnaround. We went undefeated, and we were state champs. I was an All-American, as was my teammate—and future teammate at Kentucky—Art Still. We had another star player named Darryl Lee who also made All-American. Just as Coach Hinson (who was selected as Coach of the Year) had prophesied, I went from being a good football player in the state of Florida to being one of the top one hundred football players in the country. I did this simply by making the move to Camden. This championship season also started a winning tradition that our school would build upon for many years to come. Once we bought in and

35

started having success, nothing could stop us.

We tore through our schedule that year. The last game of the regular season—played on Thanksgiving—was always the biggest for the people of Camden. Over 10,000 people attended in 1973. We beat our cross-town rival, Woodrow Wilson. For me it was business as usual. I never got too wound up about beating any one school. We had to beat everybody as far as I was concerned. My job was always to keep our guys ready to go and focused.

All the games that year weren't as close as the final scores indicated because back then, there just wasn't a whole lot of scoring. We did whatever it took to win. If it meant throwing the ball, we threw it. If we needed to run, we ran. Back then, if a team threw the ball eighteen times a game, people considered them a passing team. My, how times have changed. Now everybody's throwing the ball up and down the field. I'm not convinced it's good for the game. Everybody wants to see scoring—especially in the professional ranks—so they keep changing the rules to keep the excitement and entertainment levels up.

Ironically, I felt my former team in Florida could have beaten the state champions from Camden—even though our Camden team was really big. As far as the offensive line was concerned, Coach Hinson liked little guards who did a lot of pulling and trapping. We did have big tackles and a good-sized center, though. We also had a big quarterback. Usually, I'd just run over and beat the hell out of people.

The Best of the Best

We played with and against some other really talented players in New Jersey and the surrounding areas. A lot of times, schools around Camden would simply recruit and cherry pick the best ones. We ended up with a fullback, Frank Greene, who was six-foot-one, two hundred and forty pounds, and ran a 4.5 second forty-yard dash as a sophomore in high school. He also sported a full beard. When Coach Hinson introduced us, I thought he was somebody's dad.

There was a player at Woodrow Wilson High named Paul Hoffman. Before I arrived, he was the talk of the town. He was around six-foot-three, two hundred and ten pounds, and an incredible athlete. There was always a conversation around town about who was better—Ramsey or Hoffman? Paul had a teammate named Bill Banks who was also pretty good. Those guys beat us our junior year, but we won our senior year against them.

During this time, I competed regularly against talented players like Jim Ryan of Bishop Eustace who later went on to play linebacker for the Denver Broncos. I played against another guy named Dwight Hicks from Pennsauken High School. He was a great running back and a great defensive back. The University of Michigan recruited Hicks, Bill Banks, Art, and me very hard. Only Dwight ended up going to the Wolverines and later became part of that great San Francisco 49ers' secondary with Ronnie Lott. Bill went to Penn State, and of course, Art and I went to Kentucky.

Art Still originally was not a football player. He played basketball only. At Camden, our basketball coach was Clarence Turner—the winningest basketball coach in South Jersey history. Because our team was so good and had been for so many years, Coach Turner would literally dictate who could play football in addition to basketball. Very few people got the privilege to play sports other than basketball. If they played another sport, it was usually baseball because Coach Turner also served as the baseball coach.

Art, myself, and Darryl Lee were the three players allowed to play both basketball and football. When Art started playing football, that's when we really got to know each other. Starting out, he played tight end and inside linebacker. We called him "the Mad Stork"—after Ted Hendricks.

Darryl was just as good—if not better—as Art in football. This guy, after we won the state championship in both football and basketball, abruptly quit school. He didn't like it and just didn't want to fool with it anymore. We called him "Doc Lee." He was six-foot-seven, two hundred and sixty pounds already and a phenomenal athlete (by comparison, I was six-foot-five and weighed one hundred and ninety-five pounds). Everybody in the country was recruiting the three of us— from Bo Schembechler at Michigan to Tom Osborne from Nebraska to Woody Hayes at Ohio State. Probably seven of the ten Big Ten schools wanted us badly.

We couldn't understand how Darryl could just drop out. He was perfectly happy smoking his weed and playing his basketball in the park. Later on, he ended up taking the GED, went to Grambling, and started as a freshman. At the end of one semester, however, he returned to Camden and never went back.

Darryl then got a scholarship to a junior college in Oklahoma followed by a scholarship offer to play basketball for the University of Oklahoma. But he never even went down there. Up until fifteen years ago, the guy was still playing one-on-one basketball in the park for five bucks a pop. He was still beating guys on the court at his age and remains a legend on the Camden campus.

Every year, I'd go back to Camden and would always go by and see "Doc" because we remained good friends. I'd always give him twenty or fifty bucks, we'd go buy a bottle of MD 20/20, have a couple of drinks and relive our glory days. I can't emphasize it enough. Darryl was a phenomenal player.

My football career at Camden was transformational. What's even more important is that I developed all these life-long friendships. My center, Kenny Fisher, became one of my best friends. I still talk to him at least once a month. He went on to play with Joe Klecko at Temple.

I've remained good friends with one of my running backs also. Carl "Coco" Arline blew out his knee during his senior season. But boy, you talk about an exciting runner. Oh my goodness. Man, could this guy run. He'd go as fast left and right as he would going forward.

Another life-long friend, David "Toughskin" Stephens, was a defensive end who was a year behind Art and me. He followed us to Kentucky. Afterwards, he was drafted by the Minnesota Vikings, but he just couldn't stay focused. He remains a dear friend to this day. I'm constantly amazed by the friends I've made—and maintained—through football.

Ken Fisher—*In His Own Words*

"When I first met Derrick, he was a humble brother. I saw him not only as a real person, but as a real athlete. When a big guy who looks physically like Ben Wallace transfers in as your starting quarterback, you know you're going to have a good team. He was all about winning and doing the right thing. He was the piece of the puzzle that put us over the hump.

Derrick didn't come in bragging or trying to make friends. But he could easily talk to anyone, and he accepted everyone. He didn't come off with that type of 'I'm the man' attitude. We're talking Camden where everyone thinks they're the man. You could tell right away that he was a team player. He fit in well because we all believed in sacrificing for the good of the team.

Derrick led by example. Anyone could talk a good game, but the bottom line is playing the game. Derrick certainly did that. When he did a double-clutch dunk, or smacked somebody's jump shot into the bleachers, or threw a football the length of the football field, that's all we needed to see.

I knew we'd be successful—even that first year when we went 2 – 8. In a lot of those games, we were in a position to win. As an athlete, that's a big part of competition. You always want to be in a position to win. We proved ourselves the very next year. We were special. Somebody called us the 'Dream Team.'

Derrick still owes me for changing positions. I was previously a running back. The fact that I became his center shows you what kind of blocker I was. It also shows you how persuasive Derrick could be. I gave up being in the backfield with Derrick in order to block for him.

Off the field, Derrick kept a very low profile. He wasn't loud at all. I don't know how he behaved behind my back, but we were together all the time. He wasn't the type of guy who normally went looking for trouble.

However, I do remember Derrick getting into a couple of fights. There were always people challenging you in our neighborhood. He went up against some grown men and still handled his business. One guy was like a Joe Frazier-type dude. You handle someone like that once or twice, and people don't bother you much anymore.

I wasn't surprised at all about Derrick's success in college and the pros. If you looked at our high school team, we had seven or eight guys who went on to play at the highest levels. We had so many recruiters coming in for visits, and Derrick welcomed all of them with open arms. He didn't shun anyone. He always took time to listen to people. When Derrick wound up at Kentucky, I knew he was going to do well. Later on in my playing career, I even considered joining him there as a transfer.

Look at what Derrick accomplished while playing at Kentucky and the SEC. That should tell you what kind of quarterback he could have been in the NFL. He reminded me of James Harris at the time. He was even a much better runner than Harris. We didn't see many quarterbacks like that before that.

When you're a people person like Derrick, it's not surprising that he ended up in politics. Some people talk to you just because they're politicking. Others talk to you because they're simply keeping it real. Derrick keeps it real all the time."

<u>Another State Championship</u>

After our football state championship, I was more than ready for my senior year in basketball. We were eligible again—after sitting out the tournament the year before—and took on all prisoners. We'd play anybody who wanted to play us. Not to be outdone by football, we won the state championship in basketball as well.

We lost one game that year to Cherry Hill West. I'll never forget it. Our guys thought we could beat anybody, anytime, on any floor. A couple of our guys were drinking before the game, and that cost us. Earlier in the year, we had beaten that team by a lot. We thought we could just show up and win.

I was part of the drinking also. I didn't normally drink, but if some-one bought a bottle, I'd take a sip—just to be a part of the guys. The thing you didn't want to do is make everyone think that you're better than them. You didn't want to be some goody-goody. I wanted every-one to know that I was a guy's guy, but I also knew that Coach Hinson was a no-nonsense coach who was keeping a watchful eye out for me. I had to be very careful. I didn't want to get into trouble with him be-cause with Coach Hinson, there were no sacred goats.

Hitting the Books

Academically, I didn't have any problems adjusting to a big school. Ms. Nimmo made sure of that. Hazel Nimmo was the librarian at Camden High, and she rode herd over everyone—especially me. The first day of school, she walked up to me, introduced herself, and asked me to come see her whenever I got a break between classes.

"You're not like these other kids," she told me. "You're different. You're like me, a Southerner. We see things differently."

That was true. My nickname was "Country" because they thought I was the most country thing moving. East coast kids looked at things differently than I did. That's a fact. Ms. Nimmo told me she wanted to see all my assignments before I turned them in. In addition, she wanted me to come to the library to do research during my study hall hour ra-ther than just socializing like everybody else.

I learned very quickly how to find my way around the library. For two years, I'd sit at the front desk and help people check books in and out. Everyone got a kick out of how tall I was and how I towered over everyone passing by the front desk.

Ms. Nimmo and I had very different knowledge backgrounds. When we had to do our senior paper, I chose to do mine on the Heis-man Trophy. I thought everybody knew what the Heisman was. I told Ms. Nimmo I was going to win the thing. She had never even heard of it. I was finally able to teach Ms. Nimmo about something instead of her always teaching me.

The knowledge I gained during that period with Ms. Nimmo was invaluable. Once again, someone who I did not know saw me, singled me out, and took a personal interest in helping me.

Another person who made a huge impact on my life was Ms. McNeil. She was my homeroom teacher back in Hastings during my sophomore year. She also served as my English teacher and later became the principal of the entire school. I was her guy. She went out of her way to encourage me. Although she was less than five feet tall, she wasn't afraid to reprimand me at all when I needed it. Once, she caught me flirting with a girl in the middle of class.

"Derrick, we all think you got a chance to be and do something special," she said. "But if you keep acting up in class like that, you won't ever leave here. You'll be working in the potato fields for the rest of your life. That won't ever happen again, will it?"

It never did. Now, whenever I go home, I make sure I go see Ms. McNeil and thank her. She was one of these people who always commanded respect. But in turn, she gave you respect also. Ms. McNeil was another one of many who invested in a young Derrick Ramsey. Sometimes I can't even fathom who I am because I'm a part of all these people who contributed to my successes. Everywhere I've been, there have been people like that.

Throughout my life, I've tried to repay those people by investing in young people like everyone did with me. You want to share things that you know will help people out. You don't know what's going to stick in someone's mind or not. Things happen in my life all the time that I can reflect back to a point and remember how someone told me something good was going to happen—and then I got to see it happen and live it out. I want to do that for others. My life has been a blessing. I couldn't have ever imagined it turning out as great as it did.

Ms. Ethel McNeil—*In Her Own Words*

"I was there when Derrick started in school. I was a rookie teacher that year. Our parents and grandparents all went to the same Methodist church in Hastings, so I knew Derrick ever since he was a baby. His grandmother lived right across the street from me.

Derrick always had this drive. You could see it in him at a very young age. He was always active and at the top of his game in everything he did. There were things you could see in Derrick just by his smile. I never saw him without a smile on his face. He loved being the leader of the pack. On top of all that, Derrick was also one of the most respectful young men that anybody could ever meet.

In Hastings, we taught all our young men to be respectful. We also expected them to go to college so they wouldn't have to spend their entire lives picking potatoes. Everyone knew they had to somehow get out of town to improve their circumstances.

Still, I was really upset with Coach Hinson when he decided to take Derrick

41

away from Hastings so quickly. We all wanted him to stay because everyone knew he was one of the top people in our school. I probably cried more than his momma did. I had it out with Coach Hinson and still haven't gotten over what he did to this day. I did realize later on that it was a good thing for Derrick, though. Derrick ended up leaving us, but every single time he came back to Hastings he always made sure he paid me a visit.

I always had good rapport with Derrick and with all my students. When he was in my class, Derrick was already so big. I had to look up all the time. I'm only four-foot-nine, so sometimes I didn't know how I was going to deal with those six-foot fellows. Derrick played both basketball and football. For our little town, our athletes were just top notch.

Derrick was also a good student. All his brothers and his sister were good students too. He always had his homework done, and when he came to school, he was always dressed well and looked like a top-notch student. I knew he was headed for something special.

Derrick's daddy worked delivering gas. He was a very likable man but more importantly, he was a father who encouraged his children. His mother was the same way. Derrick looks just like his mom in my opinion. She was definitely no-nonsense, but she also liked to make people laugh. Both his parents pushed him to be the best. When Derrick came back home, he built his mother and father a new house on the other side of town.

When Derrick got married, I was shocked. He and his wife—who's a beautiful person—held their wedding ceremony in a museum, which wasn't something you normally see Black people do. It was so beautiful, though. And I was so thankful that they invited me.

I was so surprised that Derrick went into politics. I never pictured him being a politician at all. I certainly never told him to go that route. Hastings has put out some real professional people in all different areas.

As you can see, I'm still very attached to Derrick. I still have a strong connection with him. He's my special guy. Whenever anyone comes into Hastings, they'll see a big display with Derrick's face on it. I tell every one of our visitors that we got a star who represented our school with dignity and class. We need young people making a difference like Derrick did."

Choosing a College

I heeded my mom's warning and pretty much stayed out of trouble during my time at Camden. Coach Hinson knew how my parents raised me. They had always set a curfew for twelve o'clock. It didn't matter how old you were. Even when I went home as a college graduate, the curfew was still twelve o'clock. I followed the rules. In Camden, I had curfew every night at eleven o'clock, including weekends. One time I arrived back at 11:03 and the door was locked. I ended up having to stay with Coach Hinson's brother down the block that night.

I really liked the girls at Camden also. I dated a lot, but my dad would have moved mountains to make sure that what happened to him with my mom getting pregnant so young wasn't something that would happen with me. He never dwelled on it or made it a big focal point, but he just wanted to make sure that I had the best path possible in life.

All in all, I had a fabulous experience in Camden and ended my high school career in spectacular fashion. We won two state championships in the same year, with me being a vital part of both teams. Being captain of the football team also had special meaning for me. It wasn't about individual honors. I didn't care about any of that. If I can get me a state championship, I'll take that over All-State awards any day of the week. There's nothing like the satisfaction of winning.

By the time it came down to choosing a college, Art and I had already decided early on that we were going to go somewhere together. With all the competition we'd be facing, Coach Hinson felt it would be beneficial if we had each other to lean on. I had always been one to make my own decisions, so it wasn't like Art and I were joined at the hip. Even after we got to Kentucky, we ended up with separate roommates and did our own thing much of the time.

Art was perfect for me, though, as a friend and a teammate. No one worked harder than Art Still. We understood what we had to do to be competitive. But Art also happens to be one of the goofiest people you'll ever meet. We were out in California for a short time together in 1978. While walking down the street in Beverly Hills, we ran into Henry Winkler, who played Fonzie on the hit show *Happy Days*. He's not a big guy. Remember, I'm 6-foot-6 and Art's 6-foot-7 and a half, so we're towering over Fonzie. Art walks up to him, reaches his hand out and tweaks Fonzie's left nipple.

"Hey buddy," Art says in an exaggerated cartoon voice, "You're Tiny Tim."

I mean, who in the hell does that? Fonzie didn't know what to think. We probably scared the hell out of him.

Another time—when I was deputy secretary—Art, Jerry Blanton, and myself appeared on Dick Gabriel's radio show. Art was thinking of moving back to Kentucky at the time, so Dick asked him what he enjoyed most during his playing days here.

"What I miss about Kentucky is being in the shower with the guys," Art answered innocently.

As we went to commercial, I asked Art if he had lost his fricking mind. He had essentially just implied to everyone that he was gay. Art dismissed it and told me that I was acting way too serious. I told him in return that I WAS SERIOUS and to knock off the silly stuff.

When we returned on the air, Dick then asked Art about some of his fondest memories about Commonwealth Stadium.

"Well, when we're running out on the field, and they're holding the cheerleaders up in the air…," Art described.

Now I'm furious. Everyone thinks he's a fricking pervert. The guy was just always goofy. He was way too smart to always be acting that way. I told him that if he ever pulled that crap again that we were going to scramble right then and there.

Our freshman year at Kentucky, Art became a starter four or five games in. I had to play freshman ball. It really annoyed me that he would get to play before I did. I wasn't mad at him. It just meant I had to work harder, which I had no problem doing.

But that's jumping ahead a little bit. The college recruiting buzz started during our junior year of high school. Even though we only went 2 – 8, a lot of people were talking about Art, Daryl Lee, and me. Together with Bill Banks and Dwight Hicks, we were supposedly the prize of South Jersey. Everybody in the Big Ten wanted us.

Back then, you could take as many recruiting visits as you wanted. The universities paid for it all. If Michigan wanted you, they'd fly you to Ann Arbor and wine and dine you during the visit. I took visits to Michigan, Michigan State, and Minnesota. I would have taken more, but keep in mind that this was right in the middle of basketball season.

I loved it. I had never been on an airplane. I'd never been to a real restaurant. Sure, I had been to Kentucky Fried Chicken for takeout, but I never dined in at a real restaurant before. The closest I came to eating out was when we stopped at a McDonald's or White Castle while traveling with my parents as they were taking my older siblings back to college. These recruiting visits opened up a whole new world to me.

Michigan threw out the red carpet for us. They pitched us saying that at one o'clock on Saturdays, Michigan Stadium became the third largest city in the state. It was a bit intimidating. Keep in mind my background. I'm from Hastings, a tiny community of 650 people. I went to school in Camden, a modest city of perhaps 50,000 people. I played in front of 10,000 people at the Turkey game on Thanksgiving.

Now, just before kickoff, they bring us all into "The Big House" with nearly 110,000 screaming fans. My chin hit the floor. I could not believe how many people they packed into that gigantic stadium.

As daunting as that was, I knew I could play at Michigan. Their current quarterback was Dennis Franklin. Franklin was an African American, so I knew my race wouldn't be an issue. The Big Ten conference had been playing African American players forever anyway. Sandy Stephens led Minnesota to the Rose Bowl in the early '60s. Michigan State had an African American quarterback named Charlie Baggett. Ohio State had Cornelius Green, and Michigan had Franklin.

I knew when Michigan was telling me, "This could be you," that they weren't just feeding me a line.

Coach Bo Schembechler was already a legend at the time. There was a certain mystique about him because of all his success. Art and I just took it all in. We weren't going to make any spur-of-the-moment decisions. The decision was actually easier for Art than it was for me. He was either going to play linebacker like he did in high school or transition to a tight end or defensive end at the collegiate level. I, on the other hand, was dead set on playing quarterback. Coach Hinson, who shepherded us on several of these recruiting trips, was going to make sure that the school we signed with was willing to play a quarterback who looked like me.

In addition to Michigan, we visited several other Big Ten schools. The guy who took us around at Minnesota was Tony Dungy, who eventually became the first African American to win a Super Bowl when he coached the Indianapolis Colts to that 2007 championship. When you saw guys like Tony Dungy that looked like you walking around campus, then your decision came down only to if you were good enough to play there.

I didn't really consider going to any southern schools. The South at that time just wasn't ready to accept having African American quarterbacks lead their teams. One of my good friends, Condredge Holloway—who was the first African American quarterback to start in the SEC—told me about his recruiting trip to Alabama where legendary Crimson Tide coach Paul "Bear" Bryant told Condredge flat out that he was not going to play him at quarterback.

Condredge ended up having an outstanding career at Tennessee while Coach Bryant and Alabama quickly changed their stance on recruiting and playing African Americans. I'll never forget that historic clash where USC's Sam "The Bam" Cunningham and his African

American teammates at the University of Southern California dominated the Crimson Tide in a game that changed the entire landscape of college football. Shortly after that beatdown, Bryant recruited Woodrow Lowe to the University of Alabama. The next year, he recruited Willie Shelby. And as they say, the rest is history. If you can't beat them, then recruit them.

Art and I also visited HBCUs like Bethune-Cookman. I had no interest in going there—especially after the world had opened up for me. Coach Hinson and my sister had both gone there, so I visited basically as a courtesy. It was a helpful comparison to what we had seen at these other bigger schools.

We also visited Temple because it was essentially right across the street from Camden. Many of the teachers at our school were Temple graduates. One of the African American judges in Camden did everything in his power to try and get us to go there.

Although I didn't visit Grambling, one of my personal recruiting highlights was when Coach Eddie Robinson came to visit me in Hastings. We were sitting on my grandmother's porch, people were driving by, and you would have thought the Messiah had finally come to town. He was such a legendary guy. If I had not moved to Camden, I would have loved to have played for him.

My decision basically came down to Coach Hinson and the trust I had placed in him. My parents trusted him also and didn't really try to influence me one way or the other. They certainly wanted me to play closer to home, but by this time I felt like everyone had already become accustomed to the fact that I had moved away.

During a recent visit back home, my former English teacher, Ms. McNeil, told me something I never knew.

"We were all mad that Coach Hinson took you away from us," she said. "We were mad not only because we knew you would bring us more championships, but we were mad just because we lost you."

All this time, I didn't even know anybody back in Hastings had missed me at all. But maybe Ms. McNeil was right, because we never won another state championship after I left.

Wolverines to Wildcats

The year is 1974. Art and I chose to sign initially with the University of Michigan. My goal was to play both basketball and football there. Looking back, I may have thought too highly of myself. I knew I was going to be a professional athlete. I just didn't know whether it was going to be in basketball or football. Naively, I thought I was good enough to excel in either or both.

Coach Schembechler was okay with the idea of me playing both sports at first, but he later changed his mind. He told us he would let us out of our letter of intent as long as we didn't sign with another Big Ten school.

I really wanted to play basketball in addition to football. We immediately started looking for other schools as Coach Hinson called around letting these other schools know that we were not going to Michigan after all.

Coach Hinson was really comfortable with Coach Fran Curci, who had just arrived at Kentucky in 1973. Back then, coaches would tell you anything just to get you to campus. They still do. But Coach Hinson respected Coach Curci because when Coach Curci was coaching Tampa and they played Florida A&M, it was the first interracial competition in the state of Florida between a White institution and a HBCU. Coach Hinson knew Coach Curci was open to playing African American players. His quarterback at the time was Freddie Solomon, who later played wide receiver for the San Francisco 49ers.

Kentucky, however, didn't think they had a chance of landing us. On the night before national signing day, they sent running backs coach Nick Nicolau all the way up to Camden in hopes of acquiring our signatures. It came down to Kentucky and Pittsburgh, and we went with Kentucky—mainly because of Coach Hinson.

It was one of the best decisions I ever made.

Coach Andy Hinson—*In His Own Words*

"Derrick and I go way back. I was his Sunday School teacher at Mount Zion. I remember his parents would give him a nickel or dime to put in the offering every Sunday. He'd stop by the candy store and spend almost all of it. He'd leave maybe a penny for our Sunday School class.

He had two brothers who played for me before him. They played different positions. One brother was a center while the other one played offensive end, so there wasn't a whole lot of competition on the field between them. You could tell, however, that Derrick was going to be a big kid because he was growing so fast.

He lived right across the street from the football field, so when we'd kick extra points, the ball would go in his yard. Derrick would be out there playing with his little black dog. He didn't want to play any football, but he'd throw the ball back

47

over the fence so we could keep practicing. Eventually, we finally convinced him to come out for the team.

He didn't have a whole lot of competition to start out with because our first-string quarterback was a real short guy. Derrick was double his size. He was able to eventually win the top spot.

The thing that stood out to me about Derrick early on was that he had good leadership ability. He came from a great family. But physically, he was so much bigger than anyone else that people naturally were drawn to him.

Of course, my focus was on Derrick playing football. The quarterback position was a leadership position on our team, and I think being a natural leader was the reason Derrick became so set on playing quarterback. We wanted all our players to respect the quarterback position. They understood that when the quarterback was speaking, he was speaking for the head coach.

As a coach, I was demanding on Derrick. But I was demanding on everyone— including the athletes that went before him. The quarterback had so many responsibilities. I wanted to make sure Derrick was adequately prepared to handle anything that came his way. I wasn't about to let him slack off. If you get to be the quarterback, you must act like the quarterback. Not only on the field but in the community as well. It makes it much easier on the head coach if you have good kids playing for you.

Hastings had two great quarterbacks in Clewis Wright and Derrick Ramsey. I have to be careful in how I talk about each of them because up until this day, they both want me to say who was better. Let me just say that most young guys coming up in a community like Hastings have a lot of respect for the kids that played just before them. They always try to emulate their leaders from the past. It's like a hand-me-down situation.

One of the things that helped me as a coach was the fact that my college coach was an English major at Morehouse College in Atlanta. Morehouse was known for academics. My coach was very strict—a no nonsense type of guy. I grabbed a lot of the things he did and passed them on to Derrick and that bunch. They followed right in line with what we had been doing all along.

Before Derrick's freshman year in high school, they integrated the schools in Hastings. One of the things we did was we met with the coaching staff uptown at the White school beforehand. I explained to them how we handled things and what opportunities they would have to be a part of our team. It turned out that the kids we got from their program really fit in well with our kids, and we went on to win the state championship our first year we integrated. We had a great run during my time in Hastings.

When I was interviewing for the job at Camden High, I took Derrick and another player with me. They helped drive from Florida to New Jersey. We had a chance to meet some of the kids in the community, and they immediately noticed Derrick's height. Everybody seemed to be focused on his basketball ability. When they learned he could dunk the basketball, they all gravitated toward him. That helped immensely in him being accepted by his new teammates.

Convincing Derrick's mom to let him move to New Jersey was a whole different matter. What made it a little easier for me was the fact that we all attended the same church. They trusted me knowing that I was going to look out for her son and wasn't going to let him get in any trouble. They accepted the fact that we were all in this thing together.

By and large, Derrick was well behaved. We never had a discipline problem on our teams. I was a no-nonsense coach. If you're going to be a leader, you have to lead in a positive way. We stressed that with all our kids—even the little ones playing JV ball who one day would eventually step up into their own leadership roles. You have to demonstrate that you can handle pressure in order to get others to follow.

We got off to a disappointing start in Camden. Although our record was only 2 – 8 the first year, I wasn't overly concerned. The team was winless before we got there. Our two victories were very important because you could see the togetherness developing. The team cared about winning. Of course, the next year, we won the state championship.

We played Woodrow Wilson, our archrival, every Thanksgiving morning. I knew the town held a wild pep rally the night before the game. We decided we didn't want our players to be a part of that pep rally, so we made them report to the gym by 8:00 that evening. The entire team ended up sleeping together in the gym. We got up on Thanksgiving morning, had breakfast, and headed directly to the stadium to play. That's how dedicated we were.

Derrick decided he wanted to play basketball as well as football. We went and talked to the basketball coach. He had two other big kids, Art Still and Darryl Lee, playing on his team at the time. I told him that if he wanted Derrick to play basketball, then he had to allow Art and Darryl to play football also. From that point on, all three of them became two-sport stars.

Art and Derrick were like two peas in a pod when they played for me. They were both dependent on each other. Art became one of Derrick's passing targets because he was so big, and we could always find him out there—especially for the short passing game. They got along so well together. They both came from big families, so it was easy for them to be accepted by each other.

We had a lot of colleges coming by to recruit both Art and Derrick. The decision was all theirs as to which school they wanted to attend. I didn't pick out a school for them. I let people come in and talk, but they made the final decision. I went along with whatever they decided to do.

They decided on Kentucky. I knew Coach Curci. He had previously coached in

Florida and was one of the first White coaches to hire a Black coach on his staff. I remembered that and naturally gravitated toward him because I knew he was going to be fair in dealing with his players. I wanted to make sure Derrick had a fair shot as an African American quarterback at whatever school he ended up at.

I was there when Kentucky gave their recruiting pitch in front of Derrick's and Art's parents. I felt pretty confident that the assistant coach who was doing the recruiting—Coach Nicolau—was being very truthful. I made sure that he agreed that whatever position they were promising Art and Derrick was the position that they would play at Kentucky.

The worst part of college football nowadays is the recruiting part. When you go in to see a kid now, the first thing that kid wants to talk about is getting a car. He hasn't played a down yet, but he's asking if he can get a brand-new car. That kind of stuff never went well with me. We wanted to concentrate on just getting you in school, getting you a great education, and being a great team person. Those were the things that added up to victories in the end. And we made it fun also. We had a lot of laughs together out on the football field.

I wasn't surprised at all about Derrick's successes after football. I felt confident that whatever he decided to do, that he would do well at it. I'm proud of what he's accomplished as an athletics director and in his positions in state government. All his teammates and family members are extremely proud of him also. He always kept a level head. It never got in his head that he was Superman.

In the end, one of the things I'm most proud of is the fact that we were able to convince Derrick to give football a try. That was the beginning of a lot of good things for all of us."

3

University of Kentucky

Ll my friends and teammates were wondering what the hell we were doing going to a place like Kentucky. Unlike Michigan, Kentucky knew nothing about winning football games. That meant nothing to me. In my mind, I had won four state championships. I didn't think I would ever lose a football game, no matter who I ended up playing for. I figured I'd just come in and turn this damn thing around.

The fact that Kentucky was in the SEC and considered a southern school didn't bother me either. I had been through that whole race thing having lived in the South my entire life. As long as they gave me a chance to play, I'd make sure we won our share of football games. I came to Kentucky for two reasons—to get my education and to get to the NFL. Everything else was secondary.

Coach Hinson knew Art and I would look out for each other during our time in Lexington. We trusted each other inherently and knew we could lean on each other during tough times. In hindsight, Coach Hinson was absolutely right. I'm not sure either Art or I would have experienced the success we did if we had come to Kentucky alone. It was great to have a trusted friend and teammate that you could talk to about anything and not have to filter what you were saying.

Socially, the adjustment wasn't that big of a deal. I didn't turn eighteen until December of my freshman year. It wasn't like I could get in the bars, and I didn't drink anyway. Most of my focus was on academics, learning how to function effectively on campus, and just discovering how to be a good teammate.

Academically, I did well my first year. I had plenty of time to study since I wasn't playing on the varsity. I wasn't a great student but pulled a decent 3.0 or so GPA. However, things took a turn for the worse during my sophomore year. I came back that season as the starting quarterback and the big man on campus. I started going out a lot more and saw my GPA drop to 1.8 at the end of that semester.

That drop didn't sit well with my mother. When she found out, she called Coach Curci and told him that if my grades didn't improve, I'd be coming home. She didn't send me up to Kentucky to embarrass the family. After that phone call, I got the message once and for all. I quickly got my grades back on track and never had any more problems.

Lack of money wasn't a big problem for me either. I worked every summer to earn as much spending money as possible. Everybody willing to work could do the same. The university introduced the student-athletes to people who provided us with paying jobs. My first year, I worked for Feather Light Construction pouring cement blocks used on highway median strips. You talk about hard, physical labor—especially when it's ninety-five degrees outside. Come to think of it, they didn't pay us enough.

For my sophomore year, I was an Army ROTC cadet at Fort Knox. Lieutenant Colonel Kelly was my advisor and was invaluable in my progression through the ranks. He was one of the first guys outside of my UK coaches who saw something special in me. I understood why coaches frequently encouraged and complimented me. I was winning games for them. That's why I always took what coaches said to me with a grain of salt.

With Colonel Kelly, it was different. After a month of getting to know me and playing all these military board games after class, Colonel Kelly told me something astounding one day that still sticks with me after all these years.

"Son, there's no reason you won't be a general someday," he said. "You understand strategy and leverage without anybody teaching you."

I'm not sure how he came to that conclusion, but Colonel Kelly's words rang true. Even at age seventeen, I wanted to be at the top of the leaderboard while others jockeyed for position beneath me.

One of the biggest mistakes I ever made was not joining the military after my football career ended. My brother Bob was a major at the time, and I remember him advising me to complete my advanced camp and get back in the military ranks. As you'll learn later on, I was busy making real estate deals at the time and decided not to make the move. Several years later—when the real estate market went bust—it was too late.

I was thirty-seven years old by then. I went to the Army board, and they told me I was too old to join. I then went to see about coming through the back door with the Army Reserves, and they told me the same thing. It was so disappointing. You see, the military is my makeup. I'm a regimented guy who grew up on discipline. All my brothers served in the military. My brother, Ty, fought in Vietnam. My brother, Reggie, was in every conflict known to mankind during the '80s and early '90s. One of my cousins, Reggie Bassa, was a Tuskegee Airman. I know my personality, and I'm telling you I would have excelled as a member of the armed forces. I wish more than anything that I could turn the clock back.

During my time as an ROTC cadet at Fort Knox, I met this guy named Reuben Jones. Ironically, he's now one of my brother Bob's and my best friends. Unlike me, Reuben pursued the military as a career, making it all the way up to a two-star general before he retired. The current—and first African American—Secretary of Defense, Lloyd Austin, actually pinned his second star on him.

I used to tell Reuben all the time that I'd have three stars by now if I stayed with it. I dragged Reuben out of retirement to come work with me on some Black Lung funding while I was secretary. For critical legislation such as that, I needed someone who I had blind trust in.

Major General Reuben Jones, United States Army Retired—*In His Own Words*

"My first engagement with Derrick happened at a military exercise we had at Fort Knox. The first thing I noticed was how big this guy was. I heard we had someone who played football at the University of Kentucky in our unit, so I suspected right away that Derrick might just be that guy.

As he sat under this tree out in the woods, I walked over and introduced myself. I saw right away how humble he was—this giant of a guy talking to someone who was all of five-foot-five. We somehow hit it off very well. His presence stood out immediately. It seemed everyone wanted to follow him when we went out on these military exercises because he always seemed to know what he was doing. He was an inspiration to many of those who were in our unit.

As we went along our life journey after ROTC, I frequently noticed how Derrick always looked for better things for people. When he attacked a project, he attacked it with vigor. He was always sound in his judgement about how things should be and would always present a counterpoint to challenge the staff to look at things from a different angle—just to see if we could make a difference.

He was a big difference maker for me. We had so many conversations about the military, about football, and about life in general. He often talked about family and about doing the greater good for people around them. I noticed that in every single one of his endeavors—whether as a quarterback, as an athletics director, or as a cabinet secretary—Derrick exhibited the same traits that I remember made him so impressive and successful as a cadet.

Derrick was always very persuasive. Twenty-five or so years after ROTC, he was persuasive enough to convince me to come out of retirement, work for him in state government, and come to the aid of the commonwealth of Kentucky.

One day we were preparing to go to the congressional leaders in Frankfort to present some contentious legislation. Derrick offered to go first, which showed me he was willing to get out ahead on issues that may not have been popular at the time. The guy was always prepared and always made sure his team was prepared to speak with a singular voice. To see him navigate and rally his staff around various issues was so impressive. He did an excellent job approaching his constituents but more importantly, he surrounded himself with good people and put his team in a position to succeed. That's what great leadership is all about.

To this day, I still call him Mr. Secretary."

Life on the Football Field

The following year, my junior year, I served as a counselor at Camp Hillcroft up in New York, where my parents worked as chefs. It seemed I always had a gig during the summers during my time at UK. I never believed in just sitting around and wasting time.

On the practice field, I learned just how tough it was going to be at the college level. Early on, my own teammates would frequently tackle me out of bounds. I'd be down on the ground, and they would grab hold of me and purposely wrench my foot. I knew they were doing this just because of my skin color. Seriously, why the hell else would they be doing this? I'm already down on the turf. I can't go anyplace until the next play starts. It was frustrating.

The team also had these stupid freshmen initiations. Nowadays it's called hazing and most likely illegal. With underwear over our heads, they'd make us crawl through the middle of campus all the way to our freshmen dorms at Haggin Hall. During this whole time, they'd pour raw eggs and other disgusting stuff all over our bodies in front of a big audience that had gathered to watch and cheer.

After a while, I had had enough. I told Art and Jerry Blanton— another star freshman—that if anybody else poured anything on me, that they were going down. The three of us banded together, stood our ground, and for the rest of that initiation, nothing was poured our way.

Thankfully, we also had Warren Bryant watching over us. He was a year ahead of me and served as my shield of all shields. I would argue that he's the greatest offensive lineman ever to play at the University of Kentucky.

Before I officially enrolled at UK, I had come to Lexington for the first time to attend the Spring football game. I met Warren then and we sort of bonded. Our high school team had just won the state championship in basketball. In that game, I was going for a rebound, fell, and broke the middle bone in my right hand when I hit the floor. I came to Lexington with a cast on and was introduced to Warren for the first time.

"I understand you're going to be the quarterback around here at some point," he says to me. "How the hell you going to do that, and you're hurt already? If you get broken up playing against high school guys, how are you going to lead us around here?"

That was our standing joke for the next three years. Warren and I became fast friends until he sadly passed in 2021. He was my guy.

Nothing was guaranteed at Kentucky when I came on board. Understand that when schools recruited you, they always told you two lies. The first is that you're the only quarterback being recruited. The second is that if they do recruit other quarterbacks, they'll all eventually end up playing other positions.

Kentucky had recruited two other quarterbacks, and they had all arrived on campus ready to compete. Leon Murray was an African American who was totally different from me. He was five-foot-nine, a phenomenal athlete, and could run like the wind. He got hurt twice during our freshman year and eventually went on to play baseball. Billy Williams was the other recruit—a White gunslinger from West Virginia.

The very first day of practice, they listed me as—get this—number ten on the quarterback depth chart. Talk about humbling. How could I be that bad? I just kind of laughed about it. By the time we finished training camp, I had worked myself up to fourth team—behind two seniors and a junior.

Mike Fanuzzi—another New Jersey guy—was going to be the starter, and he was good. He had very quick feet, and we got along well. But this veer offense Kentucky was running wasn't designed for me. I was too big, too awkward, and everything happened too quickly for my liking. There was no way I was going to be successful running the veer. Kentucky coaches had told Coach Hinson they would be changing the offense to fit my skill set.

I also struggled in the weight room. When they checked us in as freshmen, they administered these weight tests where we had to bench press or squat a certain amount of weight. Art and I had never lifted weights before. I worked hard in the potato fields, cabbage fields, and cucumber fields, but never in the weight room.

We got in the weight room, and I got to watch other guys lift 225 pounds like it was nothing. When my turn came up to try and lift that amount of weight, they almost had to surgically remove that weight bar from my chest.

The same thing happened to Art, and we were both so embarrassed. Suffice it to say, we immediately got in the weight room and got to work. Our strength and conditioning coach at the time was Pat Etcheberry. I loved the guy. He would challenge and push you to the limit. He had been an Olympian in his younger days and knew everything about conditioning and weight training. He later went on to become one of these tennis strength and conditioning gurus working with all the big tennis stars on the pro tour. I can still hear Pat's voice in my ear.

"Derrick, you want to eat hot dogs and hamburgers for the rest of your life, or do you want to eat steak," he would scream. "You gotta get stronger. Look at your chest. You look like a woman."

Tormentor

I worked liked crazy in the weight room trying to get stronger. During that time, we had a line coach turned offensive coordinator—a former marine—by the name of Jon Mirilovich. I hated the guy. I was afraid of him and would often run all the way across the field just to avoid contact with him. Coach Mirilovich was a hard-nosed guy. I was used to his type of coaching style, but he was relentless. He drove you and drove you and drove you. And then he drove you even more. But I was hard-mouthed and stubborn too. And I never saw a fight I didn't like.

We were in the weight room one day—me, Art, and Jerry were doing up and down drills on the mat. As three of the top leaders on the team, we thought we'd just go through the motions a couple of times and then go home. Coach Mirilovich wouldn't let that happen. He kept making us repeat the drill time and time again.

"Do it again," he yelled. "Your quarterback's jacking off."

I started to get a little hot because I didn't think what he said was true. He then pulled the whole team together and said, "Men, this is your [damn] captain. I wouldn't follow him to the bathroom."

I got really hot after hearing that. He just embarrassed me in front of my teammates. I wasn't exactly sure how to respond. I knew my will had to overpower his will. This was a competition, and I wanted to beat him badly. I had to make him believe I was better than him. In hindsight, I realized it was all a psychological game on his part. At the time, I just thought he didn't like me.

After my first year in the NFL, I came back for a visit and asked Coach Mirilovich why he was on me so much during my time at Kentucky. I knew I wasn't the fastest or strongest guy on the team, but I also knew that no one outworked me either.

"You don't get it, do you, Turd?" he responded. "If I got in your [butt], what's everybody else going to do?"

He was using me to control my teammates. If he was hard on me, he was going to be twice as hard on everybody else. I never saw it that way. I just thought he didn't like me and didn't think I was working hard enough.

I did work hard enough. By the end of my college career, I don't think there were more than ten guys on my team who squatted more than I did. I put about twenty pounds of muscle on my frame also. I have Coach Mirilovich to partly thank for that.

I also learned through my center that Coach Mirilovich wasn't always talking smack behind my back. He actually told the team that I was the guy who would help them win—if everyone just gave me a chance. I considered that a huge compliment, even though he never said it to me directly.

Mirilovich was exactly right. My teammates did believe in me. I started out as the offensive captain while Jim Kovach was the defensive captain. Jim later went on to get his medical and law degrees and serves now as a professor at Stanford University. As time went on, I became the leader of both the offense and defense. The whole team suddenly became mine.

The second year after I became athletics director at Kentucky State, I fired the football coach and hired Coach Mirilovich as an assistant before I hired the new head coach. I knew I was going to hire a young head coach and I needed someone mature, tough, and relentless to control the players. He was exactly what our team needed.

Freshman Season: Watching and Waiting

Going into my freshman year, I knew I wasn't going to be playing much. I played in the freshmen games but didn't get into a single varsity contest the entire year. I was okay with that. My mission was to watch and learn as much as I could from the guys ahead of me. Come next spring, I'd be ready to beat the other guys out for the starting job.

Standing on the sidelines, I got to see firsthand how fast the college game really was. I realized the guys I read about in *Sports Illustrated* were just as big and good as advertised. I remembered a conversation back in Camden I had with Leroy Keyes—the great running back from Purdue who played for the Philadelphia Eagles. Keyes dated my Spanish teacher, Ms. Fernandez, and tried hard to talk me into going to Purdue. He told me the Big Ten was known mainly for having big linemen. The speed guys all went to the SEC. Fast forward forty years, and what he told me still rings true today.

We won our first game on the road at Virginia Tech by a score of 38 – 7. We lost our second game 16 – 3 to West Virginia in Morgantown. For the rest of season, we continue on this unpredictable, up and down trajectory.

In the last game of the season, we went down to play Tennessee. Both teams were 6 – 4 at the time. In the first quarter, Mike Fanuzzi went down with an injury. Coach Nicolau grabbed me and told me to get ready.

"Derrick, get ready," he said, "Get your motor going. You're two plays away from being the starting quarterback for the University of Kentucky."

In the second quarter, Ernie Lewis—the second-team quarterback—went down also.

"Derrick, get ready," Nicolau shouted out at me. "You're one play away from being the starting quarterback at the University of Kentucky."

I went and told Cliff Hite—the third-team quarterback—he better not go down. I was about as prepared to play as I was prepared to go to the moon that night. In my mind, I was only preparing for next spring. I wasn't ready to go into immediate battle.

Plus, this was the first time I had seen Condredge Holloway play in person, and he was over there putting on a show in front of over 100,000 people in Neyland Stadium. Tennessee, behind Holloway's magic, beat us handily 24 – 7.

After the game, I called my dad. I told him I had made a mistake coming to the SEC. I could never do the stuff I saw Holloway do that day on the field. I just wasn't that good.

"Wait a minute," my dad cautioned. "Let's talk about this. How big is Holloway? You're half a foot taller and weigh twenty pounds more than him. At his size, of course he'll be quicker than you. He better be. I think you just got yourself a little bit too excited. You'll be just fine. Just keep working."

Fast forward to the spring, and I ended up beating Cliff Hite out for the starting job. From that point forward, I always entered a game mentally prepared to play. My plan to move up the depth chart was working to perfection. By the way, Cliff went on to have a very successful coaching career after college. After coaching guys like Ben Roethlisberger, Cliff then embarked on a political career in the Ohio House of Representatives.

I also played basketball my entire freshman season for the JV team. We had an outstanding team, and I enjoyed competing on the basketball court with other talented players. The coaches allowed me to play freely, so I scored a lot of points. I never saw a shot I didn't like. I also knew we had five seniors ahead of me on the varsity that year, but I thought I'd get a chance to move up during my sophomore season.

Sophomore Season: Challenges Abound

In 1975, my sophomore football season, I was more than ready to be the starting quarterback. We beat Virginia Tech 27 – 8 on opening day in Commonwealth Stadium. A week later, we lost to Kansas at home 14 – 10. In our third consecutive home game to start the season, we tied Maryland by a score of 10 – 10.

With a 1 – 1 – 1 record, we lost our next game 10 – 3 to Penn State up in Beaver Stadium. I didn't play very well, and they decided to bench me. Then the coaches came up with this novel idea that they're going to move me to tight end. *WHAT?* I told them they could take that idea and shove it because I was out.

Word got out quickly that Ramsey was transferring. Everybody wanted an explanation. When people tried to call me, I simply wouldn't pick up the phone. I wasn't talking to anybody, not even Coach Curci. At the time, I didn't think the coaches knew what they were talking about.

I called my dad and told him I was transferring. When Coach Curci called him to explain, my dad backed me up a hundred percent.

"Derrick called me and told me he was transferring," he said to Coach Curci. "I'm going to support whatever my son says. You told him you were going to play him at quarterback. That's why he came to the University of Kentucky. All these schools wanted him to play quarterback, and he decided to come to your institution. Now you're going to bench him and move him to tight end. He's not going to go for that, nor am I."

Coach Curci responded by telling my dad all the things I was not doing properly.

"I hear you, Coach," my dad continued. "But this is how Derrick is. If you tell him his shortcomings, he'll fix them. If you want to move him to tight end, I can tell you now, he's done."

It's hard to argue with that type of logic. After speaking with my dad, Coach Curci agreed to leave me at quarterback.

Two things happened. I went back and critiqued myself. I'd been breaking down film with Coach Hinson since I was thirteen years old, so I knew what to look for. I went back and looked at all of my games. In hindsight, I could see why they made the decision to bench me. Not only was I not getting the job done, but I was awful.

I would make a good play, then misread the very next one. I would then make another big play, followed by a horrible interception. I was terribly inconsistent. It was either feast or famine. You can't win games like that. I made a deal with myself right then and there. I told myself that I would work even harder and if I ever recaptured the starting job, nobody would ever take it from me again.

We went through the season, and I didn't see things getting any better. I thought the coaches had already made up their minds about me. This was typical bullcrap on their part. They wouldn't play an African American at quarterback here, but I could immediately go play tight end. I hadn't played anything but quarterback since I was nine years old.

Here's what was strange. Although we ended up 2 – 8 – 1 that year, I could see in that team a big glimmer of hope. With a few tweaks here and there, I thought we could have been pretty damn good. Other than a 48 – 7 blowout loss to Florida, all our games were fairly close. And most of the starters were also good players from my class who would be returning.

Our team rotated starting quarterbacks for the next six weeks after they benched me. One week it was Cliff Hite. The next week it was

Mike Shutt. The week after that, it was John McGrath or Bill Tolston. During those six games, I stood patiently on the sidelines, continued to watch, and learned as much as I possibly could about SEC football. I didn't pout. I stayed engaged, worked my butt off in practice, and tried to get better. Whether I played here or someplace else in the future, my goal was to have an immediate and lasting impact.

During the Florida game, we ended up falling way behind by half-time. I started the second half and put up seven points. During that stretch, this guy named Perry Moss came up beside me on the sidelines. I didn't know who he was. Out of the blue, he tells me he once coached a guy who played just like me.

"I know you want to transfer," he said to me. "But if you give me a chance, I think we can make this work here at Kentucky. If it doesn't work, you go somewhere else and nobody's mad."

That was the second big change that happened that year. It turned out Perry Moss was Kentucky's newly hired offensive coordinator. He was replacing John Mirilovich in ten days. Kentucky had always had a pretty good defensive team. Coach Moss had been hired to ramp up the offensive side of the ball. He had coached Sandy Stephens—a virtual clone of me—when he was at Minnesota. The guy was supposedly going to change our offense to fit my abilities. All these quick reads required for the veer offense would be a thing of the past. With his new offensive schemes, no longer would my size be a liability. Essentially, Coach Curci brought Coach Moss in specifically to coach me.

Coach Moss had a huge personality. He was one of those guys who took all the air out of the room when he spoke. Previous big personalities, like Coach Mirilovich who had taken up all the air before, could now just barely breathe. We scheduled a meeting in his office at 6:00 a.m. on the Monday after our last game of the regular season.

I started that last regular-season game against Tennessee. Ironically, it was me versus Condredge in that one. We lost 17 – 13 to the Volunteers, but I held my own against Holloway—the guy who the year before had me bug-eyed. We were making good progress.

Coach Moss' offense was an abbreviated wishbone attack. We got rid of a lot of the complicated reads. Instead of me having to read the defensive tackle as part of the veer, I now focused first on the outside linebacker. It gave me a ton of extra time to make my decisions along the line of scrimmage. If our running back cut down the outside linebacker, then my read would be the strong safety. I could take the ball and be running full speed before taking him on.

Once Coach Moss got comfortable with me, he gave me a lot of latitude in calling the plays. I got to decide who got the ball. Later on, he and I connected on so many levels. I loved him and admired him. He was so smart. What he allowed me to do with the offense back then was unheard of. He'd call the plays, but I had veto power. If I wanted to change something, I could.

And I often did. I knew every player's role on every single play backwards and forwards. That allowed me to improvise. If we came up to the line and there's no middle linebacker and the two tackles are spread wide, I'd tap the center and let him know I'm following him right up the middle regardless of what play was called originally. My teammates bought into what I was doing. They trusted me completely.

On the basketball front, things weren't progressing nearly as smoothly. When the season started, I found myself playing only one or two minutes per game. With last year's senior class having graduated, I thought I should be playing a lot more. Coach Joe B. Hall told me I was still being too mechanical on the court, and he felt like I was gaining too much weight. I met with Coach Moss, and he said something rather profound.

"I gotta ask you a question, Rams," he said. "You want to be captain of the football team, or do you want to be the fifth guy off the bench for the basketball team?"

I went in immediately and told Coach Hall that I was done with basketball for good. I wanted to focus completely on football. I left the basketball team during Christmas break and never looked back.

Kentucky had a national reputation as this big basketball school, but—honestly—that didn't matter a lick to me. I just wanted to play the game. I really enjoyed and respected the guys I played with and got to know most of them fairly well. I'm still good friends with Jack "Goose" Givens and James Lee to this day. Jack and I were talking when this whole NIL deal came out. I told him, "Goose, I don't know about you. But, if there were NIL back in our day, hell, I never would have left Kentucky."

Goose was the most fundamentally sound player I ever played basketball with. His athleticism was secondary to his smarts and understanding of the game. Unlike us other brothers, he could hit free throws with uncanny accuracy. His pump fakes were legendary. Since we've both settled in Lexington, our relationship has grown immensely.

Back in the '70s, basketball and football players lived on different sides of campus. Basketball players lived in the dorms by Memorial Coliseum while football players lived by Kirwin and Blanding Towers. I didn't know if it was intentional or not, but they kept us separated. I was really the only guy who had friends on both teams—and that was because I played on both teams. I always found that interesting. It was as if people pitted us against each other.

I may be the only person in Kentucky who feels this way, but over the past twelve seasons, nine SEC schools have won national football championships. Basketball hasn't done much on the national scale. I think it's harder to win the SEC football championship than it is to win the NCAA national championship. I'm happy Kentucky has had all this success in basketball. But when you boil it all down, I firmly believe that football is still king.

Junior Season: Breakout

In 1976, our football team went 9 – 3 and were co-SEC champions. I knew we were close to breaking out, even when we lost so many games the year before. Most of the starters were in my class, so it was just a matter of us growing up together. The situation was very similar to my two years at Camden High.

Everyone was buying in to the team and to my leadership. When you're winning football games, everything else becomes secondary. Remember, many of my teammates had never played either with or against African Americans. They were feeding off strictly what they'd been told in the past. What people said wasn't all negative, but it was certainly biased. On road trips through the Deep South, I'd still hear different comments in the stadiums from the fans. They'd call you "boy" or hit you with the "N-word," especially when I started playing well against their teams.

I had gotten off to a great start that year, so the name calling intensified shortly thereafter. I scored two or three touchdowns in the 38 – 13 romp over Oregon State in the opener. We then lost to Kansas 37 – 16 in Lawrence. I discovered that even when I ventured into opposing stadiums, people knew who I was. The Jayhawks that year had this big quarterback named Nolan Cromwell. He was a helluva quarterback who later went on to play for the Rams.

I was fortunate to stay injury free during my entire junior year. When I first arrived on campus as a freshman, I had a lot of problems with ankle sprains. I had never played on artificial turf before. Running on turf on the practice fields was completely different than running on

63

natural stadium grass. For a guy my size, I made a lot of aggressive cuts, which resulted in multiple ankle injuries. I started wearing high-top shoes which solved many of the problems. Guys often made fun of my "high-top boots." After switching, I never had another injury until I banged up my shoulder in my senior year.

I also made it a point to keep my fitness levels up. My high-school coaches always told me that the better conditioned you are, the lesser chance of injuries you'll have. I've always been one of the best conditioned athletes on any team I played on.

For the fourth game of the year, we played Penn State in Commonwealth Stadium. The year before, we had lost 10 – 3 at their place. Bill Banks, my high school rival from Woodrow Wilson High, played for the Nittany Lions. They came into our place ranked No. 20 in the country at the time.

"Billy, it's just like old times," I said to Banks before the game. "We're getting ready to kick your [butt] again."

Sure enough, we beat them 22 – 6.

In the team meeting after the victory, we reviewed a play where I pitched the ball to my running back, Chris Hill, that he dropped. It was a play we had been setting up the entire game. If Chris had caught the ball, he would most likely have taken it in for the score. I was ticked off.

When the coaches asked me why I didn't pitch the ball anymore the rest of the game, I told them, "Because I wasn't back there to catch it." From that point forward, I figured I was just going to keep running the damn ball myself.

Midway through the season, Georgia humiliated us 31 – 7 in Commonwealth Stadium on Homecoming night. Chris Hill dropped the ball on the opening kickoff, Georgia recovered and went in for the score. Then Mike Siganos—who never drops the ball—fumbled a punt that led to another quick Bulldog score. Right before halftime, I went down the line and pitched the ball right into the hands of their star linebacker who took it in for still another score. All of a sudden, it's 21 – 0, and Georgia hasn't gone forty yards on offense.

That game was embarrassing. It ate at me for the next twelve months. I told all the guys throughout that entire summer to "remember Georgia."

At the end of the regular season, we had a choice of going to a bowl game that year or deferring a potential bowl appearance until the following year. Right about this time, the NCAA had placed Kentucky on probation for alleged recruiting violations. There were also reports that the team had made cash payments to players for making certain plays during games. I didn't know whether any of that was true or not. Personally, I hadn't seen any of that stuff going on. Nevertheless, the sanctions the NCAA imposed included a television ban, scholarship reductions, and the prohibition of playing in a bowl game for one year. We had to decide which year to accept the bowl ban.

President Otis Singletary, our athletics director Cliff Hagan, and Coach Curci decided that since Kentucky hadn't gone to a bowl in twenty-five years, that we were going to take the bird in the hand and go to a bowl this year. Ironically, it turned out that the one chance I had at a national championship would be next year—a year we wouldn't be eligible due to our decision. Not being able to play in the Sugar Bowl really ticked me off.

However, the quarterbacking job was growing on me. I was taking on not just team responsibilities but fan responsibilities. The first two years I was at Kentucky, I never played a single game in Commonwealth Stadium with less than 50,000 people in the stands. We were always close to a sellout every game. I knew that for us to go to a bowl was a reward to all those fans that had been so longsuffering and loyal.

The Peach Bowl invited us to play in Atlanta against the University of North Carolina. This was the game where Kentucky's fanbase first got its traveling reputation. Over 33,000 Wildcat fans followed us down to Georgia as we dominated the Tar Heels 21 – 0. It basically felt like a home game for us. Despite the flood of blue, I remember it being a bitterly cold day—probably the coldest I've ever felt on the football field.

Our defense was incredible in that game. Mike Martin was the defensive player of the game. Our running back, Rod Stewart, was MVP on the offensive side of the ball. It was a fantastic team effort overall. My parents and siblings were all there to enjoy it, so it was a particularly special time for me.

It was also special that the Peach Bowl finally signified that football was on equal footing with basketball. For years, the University of Kentucky had this incredible reputation for basketball while our football team hadn't been to a bowl in twenty-five years. Not that we competed directly with basketball, but we finally did something that hadn't been done around the commonwealth in a long, long time.

That junior year was a coming out year for me. I knew I had a bright future. I already knew I had what it took to be a professional football player. Many of the guys I played with and against in high school and college went on to become pros. I judged my talents against theirs, and I felt I was better than them. Plus, when Warren Bryant, our stud offensive tackle, came back after playing his first year in the NFL and told me, "You're there, man," I just knew I could play at the next level. My performance on the field at Kentucky my junior season validated every single expectation I had for myself.

Senior Season: More Validation

It wasn't just *MY* mindset that changed. Going into the next year, there was a different vibe in the entire state. My teammates certainly felt it. Everyone's attitude had shifted. Everyone thought we were going to be pretty dang good. We didn't let the fact that we couldn't compete for a national championship due to the sanctions affect our attitude at all. Every game we played would become a national championship game for us.

Surprisingly, the 1977 season got off to a rather lackluster start. We barely beat North Carolina and lost big to Baylor. After getting through the West Virginia fiasco and the fans booing me, we were still 2 – 1 and headed up to Happy Valley to play mighty Penn State. I knew our team needed to buckle down. The Nittany Lions were ranked No. 4 in the nation at the time. But their team was always one that I thought was more hype than performance. They had a huge reputation but little bite.

Our offense was finally beginning to play better, but our defense was so good that it didn't really matter. As I had hoped for early on, our defense covered up a lot of our offensive shortcomings. Dallas Owens and Mike Siganos both had interceptions at key times in that 24 – 20 upset win. I also learned a lot about our offensive line during that game. We were slowly but surely getting it together. That game probably cost Penn State and Joe Paterno the national championship.

The next week we returned home to play Mississippi State. That was the game where it all finally came together for our offense. We started cooking on all cylinders. We even started throwing the ball well. The year before, we had lost Randy Burke and Pete Gemmill. Felix Wilson and Dave Trosper took their places and emerged as my primary receivers. On the offensive line, we lost Dave Hopewell to injury, but Will Grant came in and secured the center position for the rest of the season.

Magic started happening for our team as we rolled over the Bull-dogs 23 – 7. Joe DiPre replaced the injured Rod Stewart at running back. Joe only had one speed—and that was HARD and HARD. But once that offensive line came together, it didn't matter who we had running the ball. Randy Brooks, Chris Hill, Fred Williams, and Chuck Servino were all more than capable.

The next three weeks, we went on a tear just clobbering people. We ventured down to Tiger Stadium and beat the crap out of No. 16 LSU 33 – 13. That was the game Art returned a blocked field goal attempt for a long touchdown. My old friend and legendary radio announcer Cawood Ledford described Art lumbering down the field in five-yard increments.

"Look at the big fella run," Cawood said.

LSU's tiny kicker was futilely chasing Art all the way to the endzone. What in the heck was he going to do to Art if he had caught him?

That game sent a message out to America that Kentucky was for real. After the game, they were interviewing Art and me down on the sidelines. Some LSU fans in the stands were shouting obscenities at us.

"You boys better get the hell out of here," they screamed. "You've already won the game. That's enough. Just get the hell out of here."

Baton Rouge with 70,000 crazy fans was always one of the toughest places for visiting teams to play. I think those folks started drinking on Tuesday and stayed drunk throughout the weekend.

The animal rights people must have also taken Saturdays off. What I mean by that is that there's this 600-pound Bengal tiger in a cage right outside the stadium tunnel. They'd shock that tiger mascot right before we took the field. They had a microphone right inside that cage. That tiger would let out the biggest roar. WHOA! After you finished peeing in your pants, you could then go out and play.

After the game finished, when we tried to board our bus to head back to the airport, a group of rowdy fans were out in the parking lot trying to tip over our bus. They were rocking our team vehicle back and forth, and the cops were standing there just laughing.

Such was life on the road in opposing stadiums—especially under the bright lights of the SEC.

We were now ranked No. 8 in the country heading into Athens for that Georgia game. Remember, this was the game I had circled and starred on my calendar because they had humiliated us the year before. We had over 400 yards of offense that day and only scored seven points. As quarterback, that's my fault. I took it personally. I didn't give a damn about how many yards I threw for or how many touchdowns I scored. At the end of the day, the only thing I cared about was whether we won the game.

Leading up to kickoff, all the fans were excited as James Brown sang the national anthem. Prince Charles of Great Britain was also in Sanford Stadium that day. How fitting it would be to embarrass the Bulldogs in front of such royalty.

Early on, I didn't play very well, and Coach Moss let me know about it. I finally settled down and ended up throwing three touchdowns and running for one more. We were whipping their butts. Once again, though, I wanted to whip them even worse to make up for our dismal showing the year before.

I got a little ticked off at Coach Curci. He had pulled me with about five minutes left in the game with us up 27 – 0. I wanted to run the score up to 50 – 0. Georgia needed to feel the embarrassment before their big home crowd that I had felt the year before.

I was mad, but in hindsight, pulling me was the smart thing to do. There was no sense risking an injury when the game was well in hand. We ended beating Georgia 33 – 0. At the time, Coach Curci didn't realize I was so upset at him for taking me out. Many years later when he found out, he good naturedly handed me a written apology.

Georgia's coach, Vince Dooley, paid us one of the nicest compliments after that victory. He said we were better than Alabama, which many regarded as the best team in the country. That, to me, went a long way—for him to speak so highly of our team.

One week later, we were back home playing Virgina Tech. I'll always remember that game. Up until then, I hadn't thrown a single interception for that entire season. Against the Hokies, I threw three interceptions in the first half.

The first one was bound to happen at some point. When you go seven or eight games without throwing a pick, it's only a matter of time before your luck runs out. Coach Moss told me it was good to get it out of my system.

After the second interception, Coach Moss told me I needed to sharpen my focus. After the third one, Coach Moss was as dumbfounded as I was.

"Hey Rams," he said as I walked over to the sidelines. "They're the team in the red. We're the team in the white."

The second half we came back strong and beat Virgina Tech 32 – 0. Again, I credited our great defense. Art and the gang were just so good that year. I ended up being the MVP. What game were they watching?

Our next game was against Vanderbilt in Nashville. Vandy, for some reason, had always been a tough game for us. This game was no different. It was close at the half, and Coach Moss was all over me for not having my head in the game. Crazy things can happen when you let the other team hang around. Vandy started playing with a confidence that they never have had before.

Coach Moss said some not so kind words to me at halftime that kind of pissed me off. He had never talked to me like that before—especially in front of my teammates. That inspired me. I ripped off a fifty-five-yard run in the first play from scrimmage to begin the second half. We went in easily and scored.

The next time we got the ball, I ripped off another run for about thirty yards. We went in and scored again. After that, I threw a long pass—and we scored once again. We ended up winning the game easily by a score of 28 – 6. Coach Moss was ecstatic afterwards, and so was I. He was somebody I trusted, cared about, and wanted to please. I knew how much he cared about me as a player, and I didn't want to let him down. I had to deliver.

Our defense continued to deliver also. They were so good at creating turnovers. I told them many times that if they got us the ball inside the twenty-yard line that we weren't kicking any damn field goals. We're scoring seven every single time. If the defense gives us such great field position, we have to score touchdowns to show our appreciation.

Florida was up next. That game was like World War III. I've never played in a more physical game in my life—either high school, college, or professional. Art broke his big toe, Jerry Blanton strained ligaments in his knee, and Rich Hayden and Mike Siganos both broke their ankles down in Gainesville. We were lucky to win that game 14 – 7.

In addition to the physicality, what made it so challenging that day was the way they designed Florida's stadium. Because the sidelines were so tight, the benches were right on top of you. The AstroTurf field was severely crowned so that if I threw an out route, I'd have to aim for my receiver's feet in order for the pass to hit him at chest level. During the game, I threw a pass to Felix Wilson that sailed so far over his head that it was caught by a guy in the stands.

As I was running off the field, his buddy next to him yelled at me, "Hey Ramsey, throw me one too!" I couldn't help but laugh.

We finally scored late in the fourth quarter to pull that one out.

As we went into the regular season finale against Tennessee, we were all banged up. Had we played the Vols two weeks earlier at full strength, we would have beaten them easily by three touchdowns. As it was, the game was close, and we squeaked by with a 21 – 17 win. Going into the game, I could barely lift my right arm due to a bruised shoulder I suffered the week earlier. Tennessee had no idea that I couldn't throw the ball.

In the first quarter, I tried throwing a deep out. The pain was excruciating. *OUCH!* I knew I wouldn't be throwing the ball after that. I had a couple of good runs early, but Tennessee played a whale of a football game. Throughout the contest, the momentum kept shifting back and forth.

Late in the game, we faced a third-and-long passing situation. The coaching staff brought Mike Deaton in, and he threw a pass that picked up the first down. He executed the play to perfection. That was all we needed. I took it from there, and we went in for the winning score.

Let me say a thing about Mike Deaton. Despite us competing for the starting quarterback job, we had zero problems with each other. We were roommates and got along well. He and I are still very good friends. I've followed his career and am very proud of what he's accomplished as a high school coach, principal, and superintendent. Even during our playing days, I was a fan of his. But I wasn't a fan of him playing in front of me. The entire team knew the pecking order. If you asked Mike, even he would have told you that I was the guy.

The Tennessee game also demonstrated how valuable a guy like Art Still was to the team. Even though he couldn't run due to his injured toe, Tennessee still ran away from his side of the field every time. Most of the time, they just ran the ball to the sidelines. Opponents wanted nothing to do with Art Still.

We finished the year 10 – 1 and undefeated in the SEC. That record has stood now for forty-seven years and counting. It probably won't be broken for a long time—maybe ever. What makes it even harder for Kentucky is that after 2024, we might be playing nine total conference games. With all the big-name programs in the SEC, that's a big disadvantage for schools like Kentucky.

What's more, if our out of conference games had been full of MAC-type opponents like they are now, I would have had a legitimate chance at winning the damn Heisman. We played a much harder schedule. We didn't schedule some blind schools of the north. We had no gimme games we could take off.

That 1977 team had come a long way. Remember that just two years earlier, we were 2 – 8 – 1. Now, we didn't think anybody could beat us.

Winners

Let me say a word about winning. Winning is something everyone aspires to do, but not everyone can do it. We did it during my four years at UK. It's not about MVP awards, glossy statistics, passing yards, or touchdowns scored. It's ultimately about winning games and leadership. To this day, the measuring stick for Kentucky Football is still our '77 team.

Under Coach Mark Stoops, I'm very pleased with where Kentucky stands as a winning program now. I wasn't happy at all with where they were before. If your program goes 6 – 6 and goes to a bowl game, what have they really accomplished in terms of winning? If they end up losing that bowl game, they end up 6 – 7. That's losing, not winning.

It's even more difficult producing a winner in a state where there simply isn't an abundance of football talent. Kentucky, a state with 4.8 million people, produces only about six or seven blue-chip athletes every year. That won't make a dent in your depth charts much at all. By comparison, a state like Florida has between 275 – 300 blue chippers per year, every year. It's much easier winning at Florida than it is at Kentucky.

I have very fond memories of my four years at Kentucky. I have dear friends that I made for life and teammates that I adore and respect. I got my degree in General Studies with an emphasis on Communications. All of us were proud of what we had accomplished both on and off the field.

If I were to go back and do it all over again, I wouldn't change a whole lot about my college athletic career. In the classroom, however, I'd definitely get my degree in economics, business, or finance. Those are the career fields I enjoyed and that would have benefited me the most in my life after football.

After I left Kentucky, the school had a rash of problems where guys on the football team were getting in trouble. The team subsequently became known as "Curci's criminals."

As embarrassing as that was to the program, for the four years I was here, we had more players selected to the Hall of Fame than in any other four years in program history. Those guys during those four years were also some of the most successful guys in their post UK careers.

We had CEOs of industry, presidents of national companies, and guys who were experts in their field of study. They all took the lessons they learned as teammates at the University of Kentucky and continued on as winners into their professional careers.

Being a winning quarterback leader under Coach Moss meant that Kentucky was my team. Before he arrived, I was just the eleventh person on the team calling plays. But when he came to the University of Kentucky, he pushed me, believed in me, and molded me into an effective leader.

This isn't being braggadocious. Even after all these years, Kentucky is still my team. When we have our football reunions, I control all the happenings there to this day. Those are my guys. I will forever be grateful to them, and I will always have affection for them. Anytime they need me, I'm there for them, just as I know they're there for me.

I'm just paying it forward. I took all of those guys under me because of what Vito "Babe" Parilli did for me. Babe was the best quarterback who ever played at UK. I was so surprised when he reached out to me early in my career. The first few times he tried to call, I hung up on him. I thought someone was pulling a cruel prank. Afterwards, I was on such a high. I called my dad immediately and told him all about it. Babe ended up being such a source of inspiration and encouragement. He showed me how important it is to share our experiences with others. Everyone can learn from the challenges we've faced.

I don't dwell much anymore on the time the home fans booed me in Commonwealth Stadium. Most people don't remember or even know about that part of my career anyway. They have no earthly idea of how I felt or what I went through as an African American quarterback. Even the UK quarterbacks who came after me—like Billy Ransdell—were shocked when they heard my story. Billy was nine years younger than me, so all he remembers about my career is me scoring touchdowns and giving him my wrist bands after the game. Whenever I told him about all the challenges I faced, he couldn't believe it.

When I told the people to all go to hell after they booed me, I got huge sacks full of mail. Some of the letters were supportive. A lot of them were hate-filled. "[Boy] shut up" or "Boy, just shut up and play, you monkey." I quit reading them after a while and threw them in the trash.

Once again, I loved my time at the University of Kentucky. I don't want to hurt anyone's feelings who's reading this. But, what happened, happened. I'm glad you're taking the time to listen to my side of the story.

Art Still—*In His Own Words*

"When Coach Hinson brought Derrick up from Florida, I first thought he was an offensive lineman of some sort. Athletically, though, we quickly learned that he had all the skills to play any position.

Even on the basketball court, Derrick could jump out of the arena. When people went up for shots, he could make them eat the ball. Back then, it was illegal to dunk. We'd have a big lead at the end of the game, and all the fans and the student body would start hollering for Derrick to dunk. We'd get on a break, they'd give him the ball, and he'd slam it like Darryl Dawkins did. That was the highlight of every game. Everybody loved it. He must have thought he was running for governor at the time.

On the football field, he'd throw the football so hard that it would split my fingers when I tried to catch it. That's how he broke everybody in. He'd throw a bullet pass and split your hand wide open so that everybody would know your place.

Derrick already had all those leadership qualities off the field, too. I used to call him a politician. I'm not surprised he ended up doing all those things he did after football. Even as a young person, Derrick was like an old soul in the way he addressed things and talked to folks. He was always straight up with all the players and coaches on the team.

With Derrick, it was never about himself. It was always about doing positive things in the community. He always looked for ways to help others. He'd take younger players under his wing and give them direction. Life's not just about ourselves but also about those coming behind us. I really respected and looked up to him in that regard.

Derrick knew exactly what he wanted—not just in sports but in life in general. He had a purpose and a game plan. I always appreciated him because what you saw was what you got. He never said one thing and then did something else behind your back. You knew exactly where he was coming from.

Derrick and I developed a special bond. When we started visiting colleges, we did it together. We had a pact that we would go to the same school. However, we never thought about going to a place like Kentucky at first. Coach Hinson was our father figure. He convinced us that going to a school like Kentucky that wasn't known for its football program could really help us stand out. I started at Kentucky as a freshman. I don't think I could have done that at some of the other schools we visited.

As a quarterback, Derrick didn't start as a freshman. Others in his situation could have easily transferred out and gone someplace else. Or they could have played another position. You have to hand it to him. He stuck to his guns and continued to work as a quarterback because that's what he knew he wanted to do.

Of course, we had some reservations about attending a southern school. There was a lot of racial stuff going on across the country at the time. But with sports, you sometimes mask a lot of what's going on in society. We played down at LSU, and you hear all those words thrown at you, but we always looked out for each other and stayed out of trouble in that regard.

Derrick had all the skills and intelligence to succeed in the NFL. Given the opportunity to play quarterback, he would have done everything he did at the University of Kentucky. It was a different time back then. I considered it an honor just playing in the league. We played against each other several times. Derrick used to take it easy on me. I thank him for that.

Derrick was always straight up. He never bit his tongue, but he was always tactful in what he said. He was all businesslike in how he approached his career. I was different—more laid back. Even in his contract negotiations, he took everything on himself. He didn't rely on agents or anything. He represented himself whereas I got ripped off by my agents. He stood up to guys like Al Davis. He knew what he wanted and went after it in a tactful way.

In terms of accomplishments both on and off the field, I'll put Derrick No. 1 on the list of all-time greats. I'll say it again. He's so unselfish. Even today, he's looking out for all of us who played with him at Kentucky. If somebody needs help, he'll be the first one on the phone. He's made a great impact in the community—not just as an athlete but as a person. That's why he's still in Lexington now."

Coach Fran Curci—*In His Own Words*

"When I played for the University of Miami, we went up against Minnesota one time. They had this big quarterback—Sandy Stephens—just like Derrick. We couldn't do a damn thing against him. We couldn't tackle him or anything. I was so impressed by the way this guy handled the team and handled himself. And sure as hell—when I'm coaching at Kentucky—here's a guy named Derrick Ramsey that looked like a repeat of this guy. I knew we had to change our whole Kentucky offense for a guy like him.

We ended up signing Derrick after he decommitted from Michigan. He definitely wanted to play quarterback, and I think he believed us when we told him he'd be playing that position at Kentucky.

I also knew Derrick wanted to play in the NFL. Before I started coaching at the University of Miami, they had never had a player make it to the professional level. We sent numerous players to the NFL after I arrived. I'm sure that weighed in on Derrick's decision to play for me. I think that groundbreaking game Miami played against Jake Gaither's Florida A&M team also showed Derrick and his high school coach—Coach Hinson—that I wasn't afraid to go against previous tradition and history.

I believe all these factors added up in bringing Derrick Ramsey to the University of Kentucky. Derrick Ramsey and Art Still are the two best players that Kentucky has ever had—and perhaps ever will have.

Derrick got a little frustrated when he first came in. He wasn't starting right away, and he should have. That's my fault. Here I had this superstar, and I wasn't using him correctly. At one point, he very seriously considered leaving the team. I would have understood if he did because we did not treat him the way we should have the first couple of years. I knew I had to do something.

Of course, we worked it out. I hired Perry Moss—a former assistant coach at Miami—who also happened to have coached Sandy Stephens up at Minnesota. Perry was fantastic. He brought stuff out of Derrick that nobody even knew he had.

You may remember, Derrick also played basketball early in his UK career. To be both a football and basketball player at Kentucky was just unheard of. Here's what happened with that. Joe Hall called me. He had a couple of injuries on his team and told me he really needed a favor from me. He knew Derrick played in high school, and the basketball team desperately needed to have another body out there. I didn't have any problem at all with that. If he could help the team, then let him play. That was my contribution to UK Basketball.

In Derrick's junior season, we go to the Peach Bowl. In hindsight, we should have gone to the Sugar Bowl the following year, but the NCAA made us choose between one or the other. This is still a very tender spot for me. But the NCAA put us on probation and kept us out of bowl competition during Derrick's senior season when we should have been competing for a championship.

I'm still very angry about the way the university handled that whole thing. When I went up to face the allegations against us, I felt pretty confident. They had some chicken[crap] things coming up like coaches taking a kid home and buying him a hamburger when he's hungry. I know that's a rule but at the same time, it's nothing. Every school in the country does the same damn thing. They just wanted to make an example out of Kentucky. Evidently, the NCAA and UK worked out a plan where if Kentucky accepted certain allegations, then the NCAA supposedly would go easy on them.

Here's the irony in all that. UK Basketball got to play in the NCAA championship in St. Louis during the supposed probation. UK Football had to stay home. This whole thing was a sham in my opinion. It still bothers me to this day. We should have gone to the Peach Bowl AND the Sugar Bowl. The whole thing was a phony deal, and they tried to blame football when it wasn't our fault at all. The NCAA was simply trying to threaten us so that all the other schools would take note. They were flexing their muscles at our expense. We never offered anybody anything.

That '77 season was quite special. I got mad at Derrick because he told the media and fans before the season started that Kentucky was going undefeated. A player can say all that crap. As his coach, I wasn't having any of it. That's the kind of talk that gets coaches fired.

Remember, we had lost our star player, Warren Bryant, to the NFL. I knew it was going to be hard replacing him. Warren had followed me up from Miami, and I remember the Miami people being really pissed. But his dad was a really special person, and he really trusted me. After Warren signed with Kentucky, we started getting a whole lot of athletes who suddenly wanted to play for us. Warren doesn't get enough credit for what he contributed to the program. Nobody was a more pleasant person to be around than Warren Bryant. Not only was he a great player, but he had a smile on his face all the time.

Earlier in the year, when the home fans were booing us against West Virginia, I thought they were booing me. Derrick seemed to take it personally, but I didn't really think too much about it. There was racial stuff going on all the time back then and even today. I never dwelled too much on it.

When I was twenty-seven years old, I interviewed for the head coaching position at the University of Tampa. Their previous coach had made a statement in the paper that as long as he was the coach, the University of Tampa would never hire a Black person. What a dumb thing to say. I told the committee that if they felt the same way as their previous coach, then they had the wrong guy if they hired me. I had no problems at all working with people different from me.

Neither did Derrick. I don't think he had a white problem or a black problem. He was just trying to be who he is, and I was just trying to be who I am. That's the way the whole damn world should be.

We went on that year to beat a bunch of good teams on the road, including Georgia. Prince Charles was at that game. The Georgia coach, Vince Dooley, called me prior to the game and asked me to present Prince Charles with a gift. So, at halftime, I sent Art Still onto the field to hand him a Kentucky jersey.

"What the hell are you doing?" Coach Dooley jokingly said to me afterwards. "I was so sick and tired of seeing that kid in our backfield that whole first half. And then you brought him out here again for the whole world to see."

We dominated Georgia that game. It wasn't even a contest. Derrick wanted to run up the score because of how bad Georgia had beaten us the year before. I told him to forget that crap. We won the game 33 – 0. That was good enough. Coaches never forget that stuff.

Derrick was so outstanding during his time here. You talk about being a leader. He was that and more for our team. When he called a play, we all knew damn well that was the right play. Here's an example. We're playing Tennessee in the last game of the year. We're trailing with three to four minutes to go. It's fourth down and three, and we're on the right hash mark on the opponent's twenty-yard line.

Derrick was wounded—he had a really bad shoulder—but Tennessee didn't know. Everybody on the Vols thought Derrick Ramsey was going to have his hands on the ball. They were all prepared to stop him. We handed the ball off to Joe Dipre, our fullback, right up the middle instead, and he went for seven yards and a first down. It was the perfect play call because all the Tennessee players were so focused on Derrick. We then went in for the score and won the game.

We have a football reunion every year, and Derrick's still the damn boss. He runs the whole show. The guy hasn't changed a bit. And the university must think just as highly of him still because he's served on the UK Board of Trustees for crying out loud. Are you kidding me? He's a very special guy.

As you know, Derrick played tight end for most of his NFL career. I told Derrick that if he went to the pros, he wasn't going to be a quarterback. It had nothing to do with black or white. You look at all those guys like Tom Brady or Bob Griese back in the day. They were passing machines. They weren't running quarterbacks. Derrick didn't have the sophisticated kind of arm that you needed in the pros. When I tried to tell him the honest truth, he just laughed. He'd probably dispute that to this day. Anyway, he's got two Super Bowl rings and he retired a rich man—what does he care?

I love Derrick like my son. Today, he's still a dominant figure in the state of Kentucky. If he had gone to Michigan, I'm sure he would have been fantastic. But they wouldn't even know who the hell he is now. He would have been just another guy who went through their program. Coming to Kentucky, though, people had never seen a player like him. He was always looking toward the future, and he had such a keen business mind. As an athletics director and as a cabinet secretary, he managed and hired the right people to get the job done. I thought he could have been a congressman. He could still be one today if he wanted to. Because of all he's accomplished both on and off the field for the state of Kentucky, he will never be forgotten."

Preparing for the NFL Draft

After the 1977 season ended, I had opportunities to play in the Senior Bowl and the East West Shrine Bowl. I was the starting quarterback for the East squad for the Shrine Bowl, but I still couldn't throw the ball well because of my injured shoulder. I played okay, but nothing great.

When the Senior Bowl rolled around, they wanted me to play tight end. I didn't want to do that, so I opted out. That's when I sensed that the world was starting to perceive me as anything but a quarterback. Everyone was still looking at me strictly as an athlete. I wasn't happy about that.

The NFL knew I wanted to play quarterback. That knowledge led to a lot of unrest on their part because they thought I was going to go to Canada to play quarterback in that league. My stock, therefore, kept falling. The NFL teams all wanted assurances that if they drafted me, then I would be amenable to playing positions other than quarterback.

Of course, I said all the right things during the negotiating process. I told them I was happy to be drafted, blah, blah, blah. But I guess my tone and tenor wasn't really in step with what I was really saying and thinking. I was torn. Sure, I wanted to be drafted. But I really wanted to play quarterback.

The rumor got out that I was going to Canada. Consequently, none of the NFL teams wanted to waste a high draft pick on me. I still thought I was good enough to be a second or third round pick, though. There were no combines during that time, but I worked out at quarterback for about four individual teams.

When draft day came around, I was all excited. I was home alone in my apartment in Lexington waiting for that phone call. I didn't have an agent at the time. With the small salaries being paid out, I couldn't afford one. I wanted to see where I was going first and how much I was going to make before I signed with anybody.

Art went off the board early. He and I had talked about this day as young teammates at Camden High School, so I was extremely happy for him being the No. 2 overall pick by the Kansas City Chiefs.

As for me, I waited and waited, but nothing happened. The second round came and went. The third round passed by without my name being called. I wondered what the hell was going on. Were they not going to draft me at all?

Early in the fifth round, I finally got a call from the Chiefs. They wanted assurances that if they drafted me that I wouldn't go to Canada. I told them I wouldn't go, but that wasn't really true in my mind. The Chiefs were perennial losers anyway. I didn't want to play for them.

Later that round, I got a call from the Oakland Raiders. They also wanted assurances that I wouldn't go to Canada if drafted. I told them I wouldn't go, but this time I meant it. To play for a team that I liked and cheered for as a kid was a dream come true. If they drafted me, I would definitely come play for them. I loved their image. That organization was built basically from Black colleges. They were the organization that drafted Eldridge Dickey, and they had a history of African American players. They had demonstrated in the past that they weren't afraid of drafting an African American athlete at quarterback.

So, Oakland selected me as the 136th overall pick in the 1978 NFL Draft. Immediately afterwards, they told me they didn't know what position they were going to play me at. I thought to myself, "Crap, here we go again."

Here's the way I looked at it. I had played quarterback my whole life. I had won playing quarterback at every level. Why shouldn't I get the chance to play quarterback in the NFL? In retrospect—and that's with two Super Bowls on my resume—*I'd give everything up to go play quarterback in Canada if I had to do it all over again.* I was committed to the quarterback position more than anything else. The fact that I didn't follow through still torments me to this day. I'd throw those Super Bowl rings in the water in a New York second and jump on the Canadian boat right now.

Condredge Holloway told me on several occasions that I could have come up to Canada and torn that league up. At the end of the day, I'm a quarterback. I'm not a damn tight end or receiver. I just played those positions because I could.

The irony in all of this is that as much as I wanted to be a quarterback, I'm not sure that would have been my dream if I were a kid growing up today. Hell, I wouldn't want to just play professional football, I'd want to run the whole damn team. I know I could have been successful if given a chance. The reality is that people who look like me still scare society. They still don't believe we belong at the table. They tell us we all have our place, but for some reason or another, I've never wanted to sit in my place.

Kindergarten graduation. Even at a very young age, I knew my job was to get to the table. *(Ramsey Archives)*

My loving and hard-working parents were married for fifty-six years. I owe everything to my mom and dad. *(Ramsey Archives)*

Throughout my life playing football, I put a lot of pressure on myself to succeed because I knew my dad lived through me. *(Ramsey Archives)*

The Ramsey siblings. Left to right: Me, Bob, Joyce, Tyrone, and Reggie. Savor the moments with loved ones. *(Ramsey Archives)*

After moving to Camden, New Jersey, my dad told me I better "make it work." I did. Our team won state championships in both football and basketball. *(Camden High School 1974 Yearbook)*

My high school principal, Ms. Cream, was married to Jersey Joe Walcott and was one of many who invested in a young Derrick Ramsey. "This isn't going to happen again, is it?" she asked me when I came up the steps to school late one time. *(Camden High School 1974 Yearbook)*

FRONT ROW: John Drummond, Vincent Williams, Harold Johnson, Eric Williams, Darryl Lee, Wayne Johnson, Arthur Still, Norris Gaither, Gary Davis, Milverton Robinson, Maurice Wilson. SECOND ROW: Kenneth Fisher, Hayward Wiggins, Stanley Wyatt, Warren Robinson, William Belcher, Nelson Robinson, Earl Collier, Eric Johnson, Kieth Platt, Derrick Ramsey.

With my Camden High School football teammates. After going 2 – 8 my first year, we returned as undefeated state champs the following season. *(Camden High School 1974 Yearbook)*

Camden's Football Coaches: Al Sherby, Andy Hinson, James Moore, Judson Gaines, Ken Dodd, Bill Simpson.

Coach Hinson (front row, second from left) loved winning. Winning wasn't an accident for him. It didn't involve luck. To him and me both, winning was a combination of hard work, commitment, attitude, and desire. *(Camden High School 1974 Yearbook)*

STANDING: Coach Wharton, Pablo Martinez, Daniel Rucker, Dave Stephens, Ronald Thompson, Robert Cox, Benjamin Hill, Eddie Daniels, Wayne Johnson, Vernon Dupree, Keith Foster, Coach Clarence Turner. KNEELING: Charles Brent, Derrick Ramsey, Darryl Lee, Arthur Still, Robert Ingram.

With my Camden High School basketball teammates. Camden High developed quite a basketball tradition over the years. Coach Turner (back row, far right) went on to become the winningest coach in South Jersey history. Thankfully, he allowed Art Still, Darryl Lee, and me to play football also. *(Camden High School 1974 Yearbook)*

Coach Fran Curci giving me all his wisdom on the UK sidelines. A lot of times, by the time I got to the huddle, I would have already changed the play. The freedom he gave me was unheard of at that time. *(UK Athletics/Ramsey Archives)*

By the time it came down to choosing a college, Art Still and I had already decided early on that we were going to go somewhere together. Art was perfect for me as a friend and a teammate. We understood what we had to do to be competitive. But Art also happens to be one of the goofiest people you'll ever meet. *(Sports Illustrated)*

Scrambling during the infamous West Virginia game at Commonwealth Stadium during my senior season. I couldn't understand how the home fans could be booing me. *(The Cats' Pause)*

Special 1977 UK Football commemorative poster. Our team that year went 10 – 1, was undefeated in the SEC, and was ranked No. 6 in the final AP poll. I was a very BAD MAN! *(Ramsey Archives)*

Sitting on the Oakland Raiders' sideline listening to quarterback Jim Plunkett—and most likely telling him to throw me the dang ball. *(Oakland Raiders/Ramsey Archives)*

A game against San Diego in 1981 where I had two touchdowns. The only problem was that Kellen Winslow scored three touchdowns for the Chargers in that same game. *(Oakland Raiders/Ramsey Archives)*

Oakland traded me to New England in 1983. In my third year with the Patriots, we got our butts whipped by the Chicago Bears in Super Bowl XX. It wasn't quite as fun being a "first loser." *(New England Patriots/Ramsey Archives)*

With the legendary Mr. Jim Host at an SEC Championship football game. He seldom cut me any slack as his deputy secretary of commerce. *(Ramsey Archives)*

As Athletics Director at Coppin State, the NCAA awarded us a grant for $900,000 that allowed me to pay for summer school for all our student athletes. That's when we shifted into high gear academically. *(NCAA Champion Magazine)*

With United States Senator Mitch McConnell. I've been given opportunities and access to people who could make a difference in our state, our country, and our world. *(Ramsey Archives)*

With my coauthor, Dr. John Huang. Thank you for your tireless efforts in helping me share my story. You get it, my friend. It's about time. *(Ramsey Archives)*

4

NFL

The average NFL career runs about 2.76 years. I was happy to start mine with the Raiders. I wasn't happy I fell to the fifth round, but I was relieved I made it to the league.

Before 1978, I had never been out to the West Coast. In January of that year, shortly before the draft, I traveled out to Los Angeles as part of an agent recruitment deal. Coming from Hastings, to Camden, to Lexington—the bright lights of LA felt really cool.

I finally made it up to Oakland for our rookie minicamp. From Lexington, I loaded up all my worldly possessions in my Corvette and drove to California. Coach John Madden and I met for the first time and developed an immediate relationship. He took a liking to me early on, but the guy was all business. John was probably the most knowledgeable coach I was ever around. And I was around a lot of great coaches throughout my career. I had no idea at the time that he was planning to retire after the season. I truly believe that my career would have been a whole lot different had I played for him longer.

Madden was a tight end coach. The Raiders at that time had great tight ends. Raymond Chester and Dave Casper were two legendary guys I learned to play the position under.

I started out alternating between tight end and wide receiver. The Raiders still weren't sure where they wanted to play me. There was even some conversation about playing defensive back or linebacker, but I sure as hell didn't want to tackle anybody. At the time, I weighed about 215 pounds and was plenty fast enough to play the speedy wide receiver slot. My big feet could move, and nobody ever ran me down from behind. I recorded runs of sixty yards or more in both college and the NFL.

Negotiating a Contract

By the time training camp rolled around, I still didn't have an official agent on the financial front. I had a guy named Doc Daniels who I thought was going to represent me. He was an interesting guy. Doc had his Ph.D., but he also had been a professional football player earlier on. I hadn't signed anything with him, but I liked him. However, once I discovered how little I'd be making salary wise, I knew I didn't have enough money to pay him as an agent. I ended up giving him a couple of thousand dollars to represent me, and we called it even. He did end up representing Art also during his contract negotiations.

I signed a five-year contract, which is what everybody in the league did at the time. As I learned later on, it wasn't really a contract but rather a commitment to indentured servitude. It was ridiculous. The contract was totally one-sided. The Raiders could cut me at any time, and I wouldn't get paid a dime. There were no guaranteed contracts to speak of.

I basically signed my services away for five years for $270,000 total. The only thing guaranteed was my signing bonus of $25,000. In 1978, I was paying $500 a month for an apartment. There just wasn't much left to go around.

During this period, seventy to eighty percent of the African American players in the National Football League came from the poverty level or below. Not much has changed today. They're still coming from the farms, the backwoods, and the inner cities. The median salary back when I started was only $48,000. The minimum salary today is $500,000 to $600,000. Yet, when I was just two years removed from the game, seventy-eight percent of the players eventually filed for bankruptcy. Despite the exorbitant salaries, that number is still over seventy percent today.

I never made $500,000 a year during the time I played. I wasn't some bench player, either. I was first alternate to the Pro Bowl twice and simply came on the scene a couple of decades too early. But I realized that if I worked hard, if I worked smart, took some chances, and minimized risk, then I could still get to where I wanted to be wealthwise. I was fortunate that I had parents who taught me how to save and manage my money.

Coach Curci drilled it in to me also. He told me so many times that I couldn't be irresponsible, that I had to save money. Hopefully I'd get to live a full life, which didn't necessarily include working my entire life.

I needed to have some time in retirement to enjoy the fruits of my labor. Coach Curci would always share with me what he was doing in business at the time. Here's a guy who only made $42,000 at his peak as head coach at Kentucky. And yet, he's been enjoying retirement for at least thirty years. He was so smart and knew a lot about money management.

The guy for the Raiders that I was negotiating my contract with was a guy named Steve Ortmayer. Kentucky fans remember him as an assistant coach for the Wildcats under Rich Brooks in the early 2000s. Steve and I became great friends over the years. But back then, he and I would go over all our contract numbers. I wasn't pleased with what I was seeing. I don't know why, but I just thought there would be a lot more money on the table. None of the players ever talked openly about their salaries. The entire time I was in football, even my roommates and closest colleagues never disclosed what they were making.

I told Steve I was going to have to go to Canada because his numbers weren't going to cut it. He set me up to discuss the situation with the Raiders' owner himself—the iconic Al Davis.

Mr. Davis and I then met for the first time. I knew of his reputation but was anxious to see if everything I had previously heard about him was true. He came into the room and introduced himself. I then proceeded to let him know why the contract numbers presented to me just weren't something I could live with.

"I understand," Mr. Davis answered. "But you told us that if the Raiders drafted you, you were NOT going to go to Canada. Now, you may not be a man of your word, but I am. If you go to Canada, you'll never play in this [damn] league!"

Upon hearing something so blunt, I figured I'd better work something out. Had I gone to Canada, Al Davis certainly had the power to keep me out of the NFL forever.

I signed with the Raiders for the mere pittance they offered me. Despite the contract, I was excited to be in the league. I immediately called my parents and told them it was a done deal. They were proud to have a son playing football at the highest level as part of the Raider family.

Oakland was a long way from Hastings, but my mom and dad would have plenty of chances to see me play. We'd have road games in Atlanta, Miami, Tampa, and all these other sites that they could get to fairly easily. Early on, when I didn't make any money, I really couldn't afford to bring them all the way out to California just to watch me play.

Rookie Lessons

The Raiders were happy with what they saw from me early on. I impressed them with my athleticism, but I didn't really know what I was doing. All I had ever known was the quarterback position. To have my hand in the dirt as a tight end was something totally foreign to me. I just watched what the guys in front of me were doing and tried to emulate them.

Training camp was interesting. Ken Stabler was one of the guys that warmed up to me immediately—or so I thought. "Snake" was an Alabama guy and called me "Kentuck." I later found out that he was more worried about me playing quarterback and taking his position than he was excited about me being there. Anyway, he was outwardly friendly to me, and we talked a lot about the rigors of playing quarterback in the SEC.

Stabler could put the ball in a dang keyhole if needed. He'd often tell his receivers that he could either hand the ball to them in the huddle or give it to them fifteen yards downfield. You could always count on the ball being right where it was supposed to be. He didn't have the strongest arm, but he was so dang accurate when he threw it. The "bomb" in Stabler's hands was a twenty-two-yard pass delivered on the money that the receiver would then take sixty yards to the house.

Jim Plunkett—not Stabler—was our starting quarterback my rookie season. I adored the guy. This was his first year with the Raiders also. The 49ers had released him before we picked him up. The guy was a tough hombre—one of the toughest quarterbacks I ever saw play the position. We used to call him "chunky" because you couldn't find any muscles in him if you tried to dissect him. He was just a big guy giving you everything he had. I'd go to war with him any day of the week.

The entire Raiders organization was like a who's who of NFL history. Of course, there was George Blanda—who played quarterback and kicked for Kentucky back in the late-40s. George and Al Davis were extremely close, so you'd always see him around the team. Amazingly, George played in the league for over twenty-five years. That longevity alone makes him a legend in my mind.

Another legend that I played with was Ray Guy. He and I were in competition for who had the biggest arm on the team. Not only was he an amazing punter and kickoff specialist, but Ray was an incredible athlete. He could punt and position any ball as well as anyone could have thrown it. During our Super Bowl in the Superdome in New Orleans, he was nailing the gondola right above the field on kick after kick. He had that kind of perfect accuracy in addition to a huge leg. He was also a fun guy to play with—a good old country boy. We called him "Ray Babes." He's still the greatest punter in NFL history and the only punter in the Hall of Fame.

Early on, I was doing everything I could to make the team. About two weeks into camp, John Madden called me into his office. I thought they were going to cut me already. I took a seat across from him.

"I'm going to share something with you," he said. "And if you tell anybody I told you this, I'm going to cut you right away. You're going to make my team. I just need you to keep doing what you're doing and don't let up."

I walked out of that office on cloud nine. And of course, I didn't tell anybody about our conversation either—not my parents, not my friends, and certainly not my teammates. Coach Madden and the Raiders carried four tight ends—Chester, Casper, Warren Bankston, and me—just to make room for me on the roster. They saw my athleticism—someone big, fast, and strong who could run with the ball.

Even though we played the same position, all of these other tight ends looked out for me. They didn't seem to view me as someone trying to take their position. They'd frequently encourage me and give me pointers. They'd good naturedly laugh at me when I got my butt kicked—which happened a lot that first year. We had these awesome defensive ends and incredible linebackers I had to go up against in practice every day. Basically, I didn't know what the hell I was doing.

Just like with my teachers at school, several of my teammates took a liking to me and helped me come along a lot faster than I normally would have or should have. When I played wide receiver, we already had Cliff Branch and Fred Biletnikoff. It seemed that all these legendary Raider greats were still there. And yet, it seems everybody made efforts to help me out.

Willie Brown was a two-time First-team All-Pro cornerback who was instrumental in teaching me how to get off the jam. Back in 1978, those defensive backs could beat you up and maul you at the line of scrimmage until the ball got in the air. There was no five-yard chuck rule. Willie would chuck me in the throat and drive me out of bounds.

"Derrick, what are you doing, Son?" Coach Madden would scream. "You're as useful to me as a damn parked car."

After practice that day, Willie showed me how to use my hands so that no one would be able to jam me. I finally learned from him how to effectively get off the ball.

I learned so much that first year. In addition to all these on-the-field techniques, I also learned how to become a pro and how to stay healthy. Realize that what players call a great pro and what fans think are great pros are totally different things. In the players' minds, a great pro is somebody who's out there for all sixteen games. The forty-five guys on the roster are depending on you to do your part every Sunday.

That year, we were playing the Washington Redskins in a preseason contest. We ran a play where I, as the tight end, ran a pass pattern over the middle. The wide receiver ran a similar pattern about five yards behind me. The quarterback threw a pass intended for the wide receiver. I jumped up and took the pass in the air. The opposing safety went under me and took my feet out completely. I fell hard, hit my head on the turf, and dropped the ball.

"Hey man, that pass was for me," Cliff Branch said to me when we got back to the sidelines. "But this should teach you an important lesson. Know where people are on the field at all times."

I never forgot that valuable lesson. If you're playing against guys like Jack Tatum and George Atkinson, you better know where they are on the field at all times if you want to survive. You can't catch every ball. There are certain balls you just have to let go.

Another lesson I learned was to not stand around the ball when a runner is tackled. Take for example when a running back rips off a fifteen-yard run. You'll notice that as soon as he's down, all the veteran players disperse. What you have to realize is that there are a bunch of big, burly offensive linemen chasing the play thinking they may get a key block. If you're still standing around the pile when one of them arrives, watch out. That big 300-pound lineman just ran fifteen yards downfield. You can bet he's going to hit somebody. Trust me, you don't want to be standing there when he decides to unload.

The speed of the game in the NFL was so much quicker than it was in college. You're playing against guys who are as big as you are physically and just as athletic if not more. You had better learn quickly.

Occasionally, you'd run into some freaks of nature—talents who were above and beyond everybody else. Lawrence Taylor and Reggie White come to mind. We used to call them "test tube babies" because they had superhuman strength and unfathomable speed. There were a lot of really good players in the league, but those two guys came from a different planet.

I caught my first NFL touchdown pass during a preseason contest. It felt great to finally contribute. My teammates all rallied around me because it was my first career touchdown. The Raiders organization always made a big deal about those situations. They gave me a game ball and made sure everyone congratulated me. That organization always celebrated its players. They were having player reunions before everyone else in the league started having them. Once a Raider, always a Raider.

If a former Raider player was having financial problems, going through a divorce, or battling substance abuse, Al Davis would give them money or pay for them to get cleaned up. If someone lost their Super Bowl ring, Al would somehow manage to buy it back for them. Fifteen years removed from their playing days, Al had no obligation to help former players out—but he always did. You'd have to search high and low to find a player who's not still committed to that organization.

Al didn't tolerate any divisiveness within the team either. There were no racial elements whatsoever. That was totally unacceptable. Davis would have gotten you out of there in a fraction of a second. In fact, I don't think I ever received even a smidgeon of discrimination from players or management due to my skin color while I was in the league.

I think the only thing that distinguished black from white during my time in the league was the use of steroids. It wasn't super prevalent, but it seemed like only White guys used them. I don't think I know five brothers who did steroids while I was in football. For the White players lacking athleticism, performance enhancing drugs served as the great equalizer on the field.

During my time living in Oakland, the baseball team played in the same stadium as the football team. One of my good friends was Dave Stewart who played for the Athletics from 1986 – 1992 and again in the 1995 season. I'd occasionally go to the afternoon businessman's special games and relax with a beer and some peanuts. Ironically, these were the years featuring Jose Conseco and Mark McGwire—two guys who have since admitted to using performance enhancing drugs.

McGwire was really strong. We worked out at the same gym. At that time, I'd consistently bench press 350 pounds. McGwire, with his big old arms, would handle that weight like it was nothing. I could just tell he was on juice.

The Raiders were also great at mentoring young guys coming into their organization. They assigned me once to mentor this young man who was just arriving on board. Both his parents only had a middle school education. I showed him how to pay bills, establish credit, and explained to him the best I could about why all this stuff was so important. I subsequently discovered that although he had a checking account and $250,000 in the bank, his bills still weren't being paid.

One day after practice, the young man came up to me all frantic. He told me that they were getting ready to repossess his car. Evidently, the car payments hadn't been made for several months. The young man assured me he had been making the payments faithfully. He pulled out his checkbook and showed me every single check he'd written for the past few months. The poor guy thought that just writing the check would automatically pay his bills. He had no idea that you had to actually tear the check from your checkbook and give it to the other party in order for them to get the money. No one had ever taught him the basics of writing a check or how the banking system worked.

At the end of the year, Coach Madden was burned out. He had poured his heart and soul into coaching the team. One thing I quickly realized was that even though he was the coach, he didn't take it upon himself to run the day-to-day team operations. Gene Upshaw and Art Shell did that. John just made sure he made all the important coaching decisions. When our season ended at 9 – 7, John called a team meeting and told us he was retiring.

John was so fun to play for. I remember a Thursday night game against the San Diego Chargers. I was on the special teams, as I was for every other regular season game that year. I approached John and told him how much I wanted to get into the regular lineup. The people back home never got to see West Coast games. This was a perfect opportunity for them to see that I actually played on an NFL roster.

That night, the Chargers kicked off and I was lined up in the wedge on the return team. The kick was a squib kick that came right to me. I picked it up and ran it forty or fifty yards all the way to the San Diego twenty-five-yard line before fumbling the ball out of bounds. The TV cameras picked up not only the play on the field but also Big John Madden running down the sidelines in pursuit of the action. When he got to me, he grabbed me, picked me up, and delivered some choice words.

"I put you in the damn game," he yelled at me with his arms flailing and spittle flying. "And then you fumble the ball. You can't be giving the ball away. Great job, Son!"

The sequence was all captured on national TV. It was the highlight of my first year. Other than special teams' situations like that, I didn't get in any other games at all. Maybe there was one series where Bankston got injured, and I was the third tight end on a short yardage situation, where I actually played a down.

I also learned during my rookie season that the NFL was strictly business. We had a kicker named Jimmy Breech who ended up missing a key chip shot field goal that cost us a game. Al Davis came into the locker room afterwards and said to him, "Get your [crap], get packed, you're out of here." Whoa! So, this is how it's done.

The transition from John Madden to Tom Flores was easy for me because Flo was my coach—the receiver coach. I enjoyed working with Tom, but he and John were two totally different personalities. John was so animated—just like you always saw him on TV with the "Wham, boom, bam." Flo, on the other hand, was someone who never got emotional. If the house was on fire, he would just calmly go about his business. He had been a quarterback backing up Len Dawson at Kansas City with their Super Bowl, and he had been a quarterback with the Raiders, so he knew the organization and the game well. We all respected him as a coach.

Regardless of who came in, we knew the organization was not going to change because the Raiders were run by Al Davis. He was at practice at least two or three days every week. He always had his fingers in the pot, including calling plays when he didn't think things were going right. That's how much influence he had on the team. Some people were scared of him. He wanted to intimidate you. And he also wanted to be intimidating on the field by always having the fastest, biggest, and meanest guys in the league.

Outside of Fred Biletnikoff, our receiving corps was like a track team. Everybody could run. Anchoring the defensive line, we had guys like Charles Philyaw, Otis Sistrunk, and John Matuszak—who later went on to compete in the World's Strongest Man competition. On the offensive side of the ball, we had massive guys like Art Shell who could also run fast. My roommate, Lindsey Mason, ended up playing at 330 pounds. My other roommate, Bruce Davis, played at 360 pounds at the end of his career. There weren't that many three-hundred-pound guys in the whole league back then. It seemed like the Raiders certainly had their share. Al Davis just loved size and speed.

Off the field, Al Davis did marketing before marketing was big in football. In 1981, when we played in the Super Bowl in New Orleans, you would have thought we were playing in Oakland. There was Oakland Raiders' stuff on every bench, billboard, and bus in town. Davis understood marketing. They called him "A.D., the genius" for a reason.

Davis always thought BIG in every aspect of life. Early in my professional career, I mentioned to him that I wanted to buy a new Cadillac for my mom.

"Kid, I don't want you to think about owning Cadillacs," he responded. "I want you to think about owning 747s."

I loved living in the Bay Area. I didn't get out to enjoy the sights too much during my rookie season, though. I knew I wasn't there to be a tourist. I was there to play football. In the summer after my rookie year, I bought my first home. I felt Oakland was where I was meant to be and would be for a while.

Super Bowl Surprise

In my second year, we went 9 – 7 again. I did okay. I finally got to play some and had a pretty good year. Warren Bankston had retired, so I was the third tight end behind Chester and Casper. Chester had a knee injury that year, so I got to play about six games in his place. We ran a lot of two tight end formations, so I was on the field a lot. I knew then that I could not just play in this league but could be an impact player—one of the better tight ends in football.

In my third year, 1980, I got to play even more. It was a magical year—the year of our Super Bowl. Individually, I had a couple of really good games playing in relief of Chester. I was in the lineup on almost all passing downs. I felt like my career was on track. Of course, I would have liked to have played even more, but Raymond was the better tight end at that time. I was acknowledged as the heir apparent. My time would come.

At that time, the best tight ends in the league were Kellen Winslow at San Diego and Ozzie Newsome at Cleveland. They also happened to be high-character people. I kept my eyes on those guys as my measuring sticks. One of my personal goals was to make the Pro Bowl. I was always chasing those two guys in the AFC.

Kellen later went on to become a successful attorney and athletics director. Ozzie became an executive vice president and general manager of the Baltimore Ravens. On the football field, you're constantly being told what to do. To me, the real test of character is about what you can accomplish when you're on your own. I have the utmost respect for guys who were great on the field and then went on to have even better careers after football.

That 1980 season was the first time I really got to experience leadership at the highest level. After five games, we were sitting at 2 – 3. Gene Upshaw called this team meeting and told us how much we had stunk it up. He then told us that we were going to come back and win six out of the next eight games, get into the playoffs, and win the damn Super Bowl.

We ended up winning nine of the remaining eleven games and went 11 – 5 in the regular season. To this day, we're the only Wild Card team to have won the Super Bowl. The results played out exactly as Upshaw had told us they would. That was player-led leadership at the highest level. You don't see that much anymore because so many guys move on with free agency and aren't around long enough to exert that type of influence. Of course, Upshaw went on to become the president of the NFL Players Association.

In the postseason, we had a great run. We beat Houston at home, Cleveland and San Diego on the road, and faced off against the Philadelphia Eagles in Super Bowl XV. The Thursday before the big game, our team was practicing at a local high school field when I stepped in a hole and turned my ankle. They numbed it with painkillers so I couldn't feel a thing. There was absolutely no way I was not going to play.

I ended up playing quite a bit as we beat the Eagles 27 – 10. That whole experience was amazing. From the age of nine, I had wanted to be a professional football player. Not only had I achieved my dreams, but then to win a Super Bowl was the highest of highs.

I had colleagues who never got to experience that. Art, for example, played twelve years in the league and never played in a playoff game, much less a Super Bowl. Jerry Blanton never played in a playoff game in his seven-year career. They both were in New Orleans living it through me. But, hell, I'm sure they wished they could live it through themselves. Winning that Super Bowl was the highlight of my professional career. To experience it with my parents and siblings in attendance made it all the more exciting.

The day after the Super Bowl, I was in agony. My ankle had swelled up and hurt like the dickens. All that pounding on the AstroTurf had taken a toll. I couldn't get my foot out of the ice bucket for several days. It was worth it though. I'd do it all over again in a second.

Jerry Blanton—*In His Own Words*

"I met Derrick for the first time during our freshman year orientation at the University of Kentucky. I thought he and Art Still were both basketball players. There was no way this gentleman at 6-foot-6 was a quarterback. I was amazed at someone with that size and skill. It was a really impressive class of 1974.

Being from Ohio, I always dreamed of playing for Ohio State. It turned out that the Buckeyes had way too many players competing for my position that year. I thought I could go to Kentucky and immediately be a starter. When the Wildcats recruited me, their pitch focused almost entirely on the basketball program. I saw all their wonderful basketball facilities and met some of the players and coaches. They told me that this was what they wanted their football program to eventually look like.

I wasn't interested in playing basketball, but a lot of our football players would later end up scrimmaging against the basketball team. We were a lot more physical, and everyone knows that football players are the best athletes anyway. Watching Art and Derrick play basketball, I realized how skilled they were on the court.

I was one of the first freshman to start on the varsity football team. Derrick played on the JV team that was destroying all their opponents. Here I was stuck on this awful varsity team. I told Coach Curci I wanted to play on the JV team with Derrick instead. It didn't matter who he was playing with or playing for, Derrick was a winner. And everyone wanted to play with a winner. It was the only time I wanted to be demoted.

Derrick could make friends with whoever he came in contact with. His leadership was about inspiring others and leading by example in order for everyone to reach a common goal. In 1974, he brought a winning attitude to the entire team. He was someone who encouraged and enabled people to reach their full potential while providing the needed support every step of the way. The guy was always positive, optimistic, and respectful to his teammates and coaches.

Every day, if you did something wrong, Coach Curci made you run the stadium steps at five in the morning. I ran those steps once, and that was enough for me. Derrick ran those steps every morning for about a year. We called him Cool Hand Luke because he was never rattled. No one could break him. He was so disciplined. He accepted punishment for every little thing that he did wrong.

Leadership becomes evident when things are not going right. It's a skill that not everyone is blessed with. It can't usually be learned or taught but rather developed through and over time. Derrick had all the qualities needed to lead—credibility, perseverance, knowledge, charisma, and passion.

Derrick was also tough. If he was going to be our leader, we knew we had to rough him up in practice even though he wore one of those red crosses on his jersey (where you weren't allowed to hit him). We didn't care if the whistle blew—we just kept hitting him and hitting him. We had to make him tougher. He would always retaliate and run the next play just as hard. He passed every test we challenged him with.

I know Derrick was discouraged early on when he wasn't playing. I remember he talked about transferring, but I'm so glad he stuck it out. It would be hard to imagine not having the friendship that we eventually established.

Derrick remembers every game he ever played in. I got hit a lot more than he did, so my memory gets kind of fuzzy. I don't recall the West Virginia game where the home fans booed him. You realized there were some prejudices around, but it didn't really hit you as hard when you were winning football games. People had prejudices everywhere. We had to just toughen up, focus on what we were there for, respect others, and hope we got the same respect in return.

I played seven years in the NFL after my UK career. I was drafted by Buffalo and was the last person cut by the Bills my rookie year. I ended up on the roster of the Kansas City Chiefs, so I had many opportunities there to go up against Derrick. It turned out that he was probably the worst special teams player I ever encountered. Derrick didn't like special teams, and it was obvious that he didn't want to be on special teams. It showed every play. Once while watching him on film on the kickoff return team, my coach stopped the film and said to me, 'Jerry, I know he's your friend, but what are you doing?' I knew I had to hit Derrick hard after that.

As an NFL tight end, Derrick was always rated very highly on the scouting report. We were instructed to beat him up coming off the line. He was a nightmare for linebackers. If he beat the linebacker, the defensive back might as well escort him to the goal line—he was that tough to tackle. He had all the tools and was so physically and mentally strong.

As a quarterback, Derrick reminded me of James Harris. He was athletic, wasn't scared to run the ball, and would certainly have been successful had he been given the opportunity.

Many years after our football careers ended, Derrick brought me on board as the deputy commissioner of Kentucky state parks while he served as deputy secretary of commerce. I was flattered and honored because I knew Derrick wouldn't hire anybody who he didn't think would work exceptionally hard and do a good job. I was the highest ranking African American in the history of Kentucky to serve in that role. It meant so much to me because it showed how much Derrick respected me.

Derrick reminds me often that he played in two Super Bowls while winning one of them. I was in a football camp in Hawaii once signing autographs. I was sitting between Derrick and Cliff Branch. Both of those gentlemen had on Super Bowl rings. People would get Derrick to sign, they would skip over me, and then go on to get Cliff Branch to sign. The next day before we went out to sign, I asked Derrick

to let me borrow his other Super Bowl ring. I ended up signing more autographs that
day than I had ever signed in my life.

We lost a lot of games in Kansas City. If losing builds character, I've got a
whole lot of damn character then. Derrick gave me an opportunity to be a winner off
the field. I've been so blessed to have him as a friend."

Proving My Worth

The next year—year four (1981)—I was ready to go. I started twelve
games that year and set a club receiving record for tight ends with 52
receptions and four touchdowns. In our game against the Chargers,
Kellen Winslow scored three touchdowns while I had two. I knew I
had arrived.

Although we only went 7 – 9 that year, you have to understand that
coming off a Super Bowl, your team will likely have the toughest schedule. Injuries also frequently come into play and people are always
gunning for you. Playing for the Raiders, we never went into a stadium
where we weren't booed loudly. Being Super Bowl champs just made
them boo louder.

I ended up being first alternate to the Pro Bowl that year. That en-
sured in my mind that I was capable of playing at the level of the best
of the best.

In 1982—the strike shortened season—things started to go sour
with me and the Raiders. The bottom line was that I wanted them to
pay me what I was worth. I thought I had a legitimate argument for
earning a top salary. I wanted a new contract while Al Davis just
wanted to add years on to my current contract. That wasn't good
enough for me because I wanted them to pay me now—not two years
from now.

I didn't think I was asking for anything ridiculous. All I requested
was for me to be within ten or fifteen percent of what Kellen Winslow
and Ozzie Newsome were making. After all, they had made the Pro
Bowl and I hadn't.

Just as we were getting into all my contract talks, I had a knee injury
during the preseason that set me back. The team doctor told me that I
needed to have surgery to repair my ACL. My trainer, George Ander-
son—whom I respected and trusted—told me otherwise. He said my
knee had always been loose, and all I needed was to let it quiet down
with some rest.

When Al Davis heard I decided against having surgery, he was livid.

"I pay one of the best doctors in the world to take care of you, and now you think you know more than he does," Davis said to me. "So, you're the doctor now."

I wasn't the doctor, but I knew my body better than anyone else.

The next week at practice, I was standing on the sidelines and Davis came up to me.

"How're you doing, doctor?" he asked sarcastically.

Due to the strike, my knee was able to heal. I was getting treatment on it, and the six weeks of added rest did wonders. By the time we came back, I felt great and was ready to go. When I got to the huddle with the first team, Coach Flores told me Todd Christensen was taking my place. It turned out that Al Davis wanted Christensen as his starting tight end.

Our team policy was that you couldn't lose your starting job to an injury. When I found out they benched me in opposition to their own policy, I didn't care what anybody thought anymore and just started doing my own thing. I practiced when I wanted and just stood around when I didn't want to. Davis and his minions were treating me this way simply because of the contract dispute. I wasn't going to give in.

Consequently, I went through that entire season not playing much at all. This was Al Davis' way of decreasing my perceived value to the team while thinking he was also teaching me a lesson. I wasn't having any of it. I knew what was best for me, so I told Davis and Flores that if I couldn't compete for the starting job, I wanted to be traded immediately.

"Kid, everybody wants to play for the Raiders," Davis replied to me. "Do you realize how many people would love to be in your position?"

Davis thought even the Martians wanted to play for the Raiders.

The reality was that I played behind two of the best tight ends in football. I wasn't playing behind Todd Christensen. Nothing against Todd—he and I were friends—it's just that I was better, and everyone knew it. Still, they made the decision the following season to go with Todd. So, I decided that I was out. I still showed up for practice but just sat on my helmet the whole time. Look—whether in sports, business, or life—I've got no problem if you beat me out. But if you get things handed to you without earning it, then you won't ever get respect from me. During the 1983 season opener against Cincinnati, I simply refused to go in the game.

"I don't care where you go," Davis said to me on the sidelines afterwards. "I just want you out of here."

Immediately after that, I reached out to my good friend, Lou Erber, who used to be one of my former coaches with the Raiders. He was now the offensive coordinator for the New England Patriots and was instrumental in getting me a trade opportunity. Mike Haynes was holding out for New England, so they traded him and their back-up tight end for me and a draft pick.

Patriot Games

I was so happy I was able to force the trade to New England. I wanted to make sure I went somewhere where I knew somebody like Lou who appreciated my talents. So many times, a team would send you somewhere that they knew you would be ineffective. I respected and admired Al Davis for what he had done with the Raiders, but I also respected myself and my abilities. I played football because I wanted to—not because I had to. I didn't need Al Davis and football to prove my worth. I could be just as successful with another team—or in something else altogether, even if I never played football.

I had a pretty good year with the Patriots with six touchdowns on 24 catches. Financially, I went from making $70,000 a year to making $330,000 the next year. You tell me if I made the right decision or not to leave the Raiders. On top of that, my three-year contract was also guaranteed with a lot of realistic incentives built in.

By this time, I felt like I needed and could finally afford an agent. I hired a guy by the name of Mike Sullivan who was excellent. Mike was an attorney and an accountant. He and I understood each other because I've always been a fiscally responsible type of individual. I started early on reading tax codes and learning as much as I could about tax law. I was acutely aware of how people in the entertainment and sports industry who made a lot of money frequently had IRS issues. Consequently, I was always very diligent about managing my own money. I'd take only what I needed to live off of and defer and save the rest.

In 1984, not only was I making a much higher salary, but I also made an additional $164,000 in incentives. That was unheard of back then because most of the built-in incentives were simply not achievable. No rookie was ever going to be league MVP or make the Pro Bowl. The system wasn't set up for players to readily succeed.

I essentially had the best year of my NFL career that year. I started 13 games, caught 66 passes, and scored seven touchdowns. Once again, I just missed out on the Pro Bowl. But the other guys—Ozzie Newsome and Todd Christensen—had bigger numbers, and selection to the Pro Bowl was all about numbers.

I was looking forward to a big year in 1985 when I pulled a groin muscle in training camp. That injury really set me back. I couldn't move laterally without excruciating pain. Then during the regular season, I injured my hamstring. Some guy came up to me offering some "juice." When I found out he meant banned steroids, I told him to hit the road. Although it ended up being my second Super Bowl year, it was bittersweet for me because I never felt really healthy.

That was also the year New England changed head coaches. They fired Ron Meyer and brought in Raymond Berry. Coach Meyer and I had a great relationship. He reminded me a lot of Coach Curci. When you know a coach cares about you, you tend to put it all on the line for them. Coach Meyer was someone I trusted, respected, and loved.

My relationship with Coach Berry was something altogether different. I was excited when they first hired him because my dad was a big Colts fan and I remember as a little boy watching Berry play every Sunday. He was a Hall of Famer who would surely help me get to the next level. Boy, was I wrong. This was the first time in my football career I ever played for a head coach that I didn't get along with. We didn't see eye to eye on a lot of issues, some of which I'll take the blame for.

Coming from the Raiders, the player was always right. Al Davis had secured that kind of team mentality. He always sided with the players. New England was completely different. Berry was an old-style coach. In his mind, his way was always right. Although to be fair, with my personality, I didn't always make it easy for him, even the few times he was actually right. I still thought I could play and be one of the best players in the league at my position. I just never bought in on how he was coaching the team. Throughout the year, he and I would butt heads on all sorts of different issues.

Let me put it this way. Raymond Berry would have been a much better college coach than he was a professional coach. Some personality types just don't mesh well with professional athletes. It doesn't mean they're not quality coaches. Look at guys like Rick Pitino, Steve Spurrier, and Nick Saban. They excelled in college but couldn't succeed at the professional level.

In 1986, I didn't play at all. I had an acupuncture procedure on my leg which subsequently got infected. I then had surgery on that area in the summer. The Patriots decided to release me, but they still had to pay me $380,000 dollars—so it wasn't all bad.

Jalica

One really good thing about my New England experience was meeting my future wife, Jalica (Li), in October of 1983. One of my teammates who knew her family well introduced us. My mom told me immediately that Li was the one for me, but I didn't believe her. I already had my mom and my sister as the women in my life. I didn't think I needed a wife.

At that time in my life, gaining wealth was my top priority. Wealth meant security, and security always came first. My biggest fear in life has always been being poor again. Hence, if I had to work fifteen hours a day, that's what I'd do. There was nothing I couldn't achieve if I were willing to put in the work. Marriage could always wait.

Upon leaving the Patriots, I was kind of pissed off at everybody. I didn't like the New England area and thought it was the most racist place I had ever been. Compared to the Raiders, I thought the Patriots' organization was garbage at that time. The only thing good about New England was Li and her family. Even though I knew she was very special, nothing became of our relationship because I just wasn't seeking a partner at that time in my life.

Then twenty years later in 2006, Li and I reconnected. My brother-in-law, Sean Jones—the big defensive end who played for Green Bay and the Raiders—called me and told me Li wanted to talk with me. I was hesitant. She was married at the time, I was working in politics for Governor Ernie Fletcher, and I didn't need any additional relationship headaches.

Li, however, was going through a divorce at the time, so I reluctantly told Sean to have her call me. Li was a flight attendant. At the time, she was flying with American Airlines, so she flew down the very next day. We had lunch, hit it off again, and have been together ever since. We got married in 2010. My mom was absolutely right. I just wish she was there to witness it.

Our wedding venue was rather unique. My sister's husband was deputy mayor of St. Augustine at the time. He was able to secure this museum for us to hold our ceremony. I didn't want anything too elaborate. Actually, I didn't want anything at all, but this was kind of my compromise with Li. It turned out beautifully. We ended up with maybe sixty or seventy people there. Understand, my parents got married at the justice of the peace. They tied the knot at lunchtime and went immediately back to work.

As I reflect back, I do wish I had married Li right when we first met. I would have liked to have had five or six kids with her. I come from a big family. She comes from a family of six girls and one boy. It would have been nice to have a family who could have enjoyed the riches that I wanted them to have.

Time to Move On

In 1987, I was thinking it was time to move on to the next phase of my life. However, Coach Meyer was hired on by the Indianapolis Colts, and he wanted me to come back and play for him again. Because of our previous relationship, I agreed. That was a poor decision on my part because I had a chance to go to the San Francisco 49ers or perhaps even back to the Raiders. I went with Coach Meyer due to familiarity, instead. Once I got to Indianapolis, I realized he wasn't really the one calling the shots in that organization.

The Colts traded me quickly to Detroit, and I finished my football career with the Lions on injured reserve. There was no grand announcement or official retirement ceremony. I just rode quietly off into the sunset.

As I look back on my nine-year NFL career, I ask myself if I would have liked for it to have been better. Absolutely. Don't get me wrong, nothing was horrible about it. Remember, I've got a Super Bowl ring. But I was also a lot better athlete than I was able to demonstrate with my performance on the field.

I also learned a lot in the league—not just about football but about people. John Madden told me once that if I ever got into coaching at the professional level, the job would involve managing personalities rather than drawing up Xs and Os. Because at the top levels in this profession, everybody's big, strong, fast, and understands the game. You have to be able to get into their heads to be successful. Like many other things we talked about, John Madden was right about that.

I got to see John's words in action one day. We were playing the Cincinnati Bengals, and Jack Tatum's mom was flying in to watch her son play. Jack had gotten his hair cut that morning and refused to put on his helmet for Saturday's practice. He didn't want to mess up his "do" before seeing his momma. Rather than forcing Jack to put his helmet on, John gathered the team together in a big circle.

"I don't want nobody to mess with Jack's hair," he said. "Jack's got his 'do' done, he's going to see Momma, so we all want his 'do' to be right."

Of course, everybody immediately jumped on Jack and messed up his hair. John had the authority to do whatever he wanted in that situation. He could have forced Jack's hand. Instead, he defused the situation with his clever people management skills. I would always remember that lesson while dealing with challenging situations throughout my post NFL career.

Football gave me so many opportunities, but it wasn't hard for me to give it up at all. After I won that Super Bowl, the world just looked different to me. At age twenty-four, I had already accomplished everything I dreamed of as a little kid. Like I had told Al Davis, I played football because I loved it, not because I had to.

It was time to move on to something else.

5

Life After Football

When I got to New England, I was already doing business deals on the West Coast. That wasn't something the Patriots' franchise smiled on. They wanted you to focus on football only. Well, when the average NFL career is less than three years—and I was already way past the average—it was wise for me to start planning for my future after football.

In football, you never know about injuries and how long you might be able to play. There are a lot of things that are out of your control. Ever since I got into the league, I always wanted to have control over the things that I could. And life after my football career ended was something I definitely could control.

Doing the Deals

I respected the guys in the league who had awesome careers while simultaneously having plans for what they were going to do next. I was going to be like them. So, in 1981, I started buying up some properties in the Bay Area. I had watched my mom acquire several properties previously in Florida, so I just expanded what she was doing to a much larger scale. My teammate, Raymond Chester, ran a real estate company. I bought into that company and learned a lot about the business through some quality on-the-job training.

Another one of my teammates, Kenny Hill, went to school with Dave Thomas' (the Wendy's founder's) daughter. Three weeks or so after I was traded to the Patriots, Kenny called me with this opportunity to buy into these Wendy's hamburger franchises down in Orange County. The problem was that I needed to come up with $50,000 in two days in order to beat the deadline in becoming a limited partner.

I went directly to the Patriots to ask for the money. This was my contract year, and I had gotten off to a pretty good start. So, I went to see Pat Sullivan, the Patriots' general manager. He called over to the bank and they had the cashier's check for me that afternoon.

We ended up with three stores—our most profitable one was on Long Beach State's campus. Our biggest mistake, however, was not building more stores at the start. Had we expanded our footprint, we would have made a pile more money. I mean we did okay—but most of the money we made initially we put right back into the stores. It took us about seven years to break even. The good news was that for the next twenty-five years—until we sold them about three years ago—it was nice going to the mailbox every month and getting that check.

Meanwhile, the real estate gig with Raymond became quite profitable. I've always enjoyed negotiations and making deals. At one point, I had acquired about eighty-seven units—houses, apartment buildings, and duplexes all on the West Coast. Some offseasons, I would make more in rents off of these properties and real estate than I did with my NFL salary.

Then came October 17, 1989, and the Loma Prieta earthquake that struck the San Francisco Bay Area causing extensive structural damage. By the end of that year, property values had dropped fifteen to twenty percent due to the destruction. By the following summer, they plummeted another twenty-five percent. Whereas before we were making a lot of money, now we all had to scramble just to stay in business.

On top of that, most of my properties were low-income properties. I was renting primarily to people living in government subsidized housing. The government would pay most of their housing costs depending on their income levels. For some folks really down on their luck, social services would sometimes pick up a hundred percent of the tab.

I didn't just blindly buy up these low-income units either. I would carefully follow the city plans and determine possible profitable areas based on the traffic patterns. I knew some of the areas were high risk, but they were also located directly in a corridor from the airport straight up to the hills—where all the money was in Oakland. I knew the city would never let these rich folks feel like they were in danger traveling through these neighborhoods to their million-dollar homes.

I had excellent credit and great banking relationships, so I started buying up any available and foreclosed properties right and left. My goal was to get to about 250 units and then refinance one of them every year. As long as they appreciated in value, I'd be rolling along just fine.

Once the earthquake hit and then the crack epidemic came on the scene, everything changed. These neighborhoods got flooded with criminal activity. You had to act fast. If you didn't get there in time to collect your rent, the drug dealer would get all your money—and you'd be stuck. Laws in California favored the tenant more than the landlord. An unscrupulous tenant could easily hold you up and not pay you for six months straight. It became harder and harder to evict deadbeats from your properties.

The real estate market stayed down and didn't come back until around 1994. By then, I had had enough of the down market and tenants who didn't pay. I decided to sell it all—at big discounts—and move back to Kentucky and essentially start over.

I remember thinking to myself at the time, "How in the hell did this happen?" By age twenty-nine, I was a millionaire. By age thirty-seven, I was looking to start over financially. I had made a ton of money and just as quickly lost a ton of money. Here's the thing. If I had kept those properties and managed them properly—even with the economic downturn—I'm sure they'd easily be worth tens of millions of dollars or more today.

Sure, it hurt me emotionally to have to start over, but the lessons I learned in those seven years in real estate would be invaluable. In everything I do, I think there's something to be learned. Whether it's good, bad, or indifferent, there's always something you can apply down the road.

I got in trouble financially because I wouldn't let go. As a businessman, you can't fall in love with your product. I fell in love with all my properties. Here I was—young, ambitious, and moving at 200 miles per hour. I was leverage buying right and left on my credit alone and took on way too much too fast. I had never seen a down market. When one finally hit, it caught me totally off guard.

In retrospect, I was way too aggressive in my approach. But if I had the opportunity, I'd jump at the chance to do it all over again. Knowing what I know now, there's not a doubt in my mind that I'd proceed much more cautiously and end up with a totally different result.

Raymond Chester—*In His Own Words*

"When Derrick came on with the Raiders, everyone was impressed with his size,

height, and his football credentials, but what really stood out was his great talent. Plus, he was super intelligent. You only had to tell him something one time, and he would get it. He never missed anything on the field and showed an exceptional aptitude for playing the game. That translated to him picking up the nomenclature and all the stuff about the game so quickly.

Realize also that Derrick brought a lot with him when he came. I didn't really follow the SEC that much when I was playing, so I was shocked when I found out he was a quarterback. A lot of people looked at him and questioned what position he would play. He's big and tall and lean. Are we going to play him at wide receiver, or are we going to try him at quarterback?

Sadly, the quarterback situation with Derrick was the same as it was with so many of the other really super talented Black athletes that came to the NFL in our era. He never really got the opportunity to even compete at the quarterback position. That's a shame because it only took a couple of practices watching him throw and catch that you realized he had this extraordinary athletic ability. The guys on our team used to call him "inhuman." He had this quarterback skill set that was so unique—the size, speed, power, footwork, jumping ability, and the arm strength combined with this super intelligent mind.

Here you've got a guy who has all these God-given gifts to physically and mentally play the game. Then you add on what the Raiders called "the will to win." How badly does a person want to win and how badly are they willing to compete in order to win? Derrick had an unfathomable will to win.

That wasn't all. In the NFL we have a saying: As a player in the league, you have good Sundays, bad Sundays, and every Sundays. Some players look great in practice, but what happens when they show up on Sunday for gameday? Derrick showed up every Sunday and met every challenge head on. On the biggest stage imaginable, he rose to the occasion. If he got punched in the mouth, he got right back on his feet. He had that toughness and that willingness to compete you see so often with champions.

It's a tragedy that racial barriers that still exist in the NFL today prevented so many great players like Derrick from excelling at certain positions you know they could have been tremendously successful at. It's pathetic that it's taken the league so long to move away from that type of racism. Even though there were quite a few Black players on our roster, many of them were still restricted from playing certain positions. We were all relegated to the offensive and defensive lines, perhaps the cornerback position, and the receiver slots. That was pretty much it. The quarterback position was reserved for White guys only.

Derrick and I are best friends, but when we competed against each other, you'd never know it. As the veteran player, I loved it because as iron sharpens iron, so does one man sharpen another. While I was imparting some of my experience and knowledge on Derrick, he was making me better also. Just because a player is young and inexperienced doesn't mean he's no use to the older guy. He helped me become a better player every single day.

I was really strong and therefore a good power blocker. I was a wrestler in my earlier days. Derrick, on the other hand, had really athletic feet. He was a basketball player with jumping ability that I didn't have. Just as I had to work on my agility, he had to learn how to power block. When it came to blocking his man, Derrick's height was frequently a disadvantage he had to learn how to leverage. We both also had great hands, but Derrick had to learn how to position his hands in order to catch balls from all different angles.

We each recognized the other's strong points and were anxious to improve our weaknesses to match the other person's strengths. We were both unselfish—willing to help each other out—while watching and studying the game from all different angles in order to improve.

Although we were competing for the same job, there was no jealousy on my end. Once I saw how good Derrick was, I knew he would eventually win out. What I wanted to convey to him was that he actually had to earn it from me. I wasn't giving him anything without a fight. I loved the process. In the process of him pushing me and me trying to hold him off, it made both of us so much better. It put the Raiders in a position where we had the best tight ends in the damn world.

You can practice, train, and talk all you want, but there comes a time when you just have to go out on the field and learn by playing. Every opportunity Derrick got to play in a game he would develop his own technique and his own style of play— and he excelled at it. On top of all that, he was durable. As tight ends in our era, we had to do everything. We had to fight our way off the line, block defensive ends and linebackers, and run every route that the wide receivers ran. We also had to catch balls in the middle of a crowded field. Derrick did it all and remained standing through the entire grueling process.

It's interesting how Derrick approached his contract dispute with the Raiders. He had already watched the same thing happen to me. Remember, Al Davis traded me in the prime of my career—sentenced me to five years of hard labor in Baltimore—simply because I demanded the salary I thought I was entitled to. We talked about it a lot, and Derrick did what he had to do. He knew what other players in similar situations were making, and he fully knew the risks he was taking pushing the envelope with respect to his contract. He was one of the few players brave and confident enough to challenge Al Davis—something Davis certainly was not used to seeing.

For two guys who competed as hard as we did against each other every day, Derrick and I still ended up with a tremendous amount of respect and love for each other. We were brothers. I knew his parents, and he knew my family as well. We tra-

veled together, we did things together in the offseason, and we worked together in real estate outside of our lives in football. There's nothing I wouldn't do for Derrick. I'm confident he would do the same for me.

Both Derrick and I came from poor families, but we both had great parents. My dad was high school educated as was Derrick's. My mom was a great inspiration to me as was his mom to him. We both had older siblings who served as great examples. Both our families understood the value of a good education. Integrity, work ethic, cleanliness, physical fitness, and discipline were fully expected within each of our households.

Derrick and I both knew what we wanted out of life. We didn't look at football as a lifelong career. It was just a steppingstone. The average football career lasts less than three years. We knew we had a short window to make money in football, and we wanted to make sure we properly invested the money we made.

That's why we both looked for other business opportunities outside of football. I bought my first retail store in Oakland when I was twenty-three years old. When I became interested in real estate, I went back to real estate school, earned my real estate and securities licenses, and went to work with a friend in a small real estate company. Our goal was to organize athletes like Derrick, put together some partnerships, and formulate syndicates to buy up properties. We collectively bought a shopping center and expanded out from there.

Derrick got wind of what we were doing and thought it was awesome. It was exactly what he had wanted to do. We just clicked together as business partners. We saved our money, didn't do anything stupid, and just started buying more and more properties. We connected with some good and honest real estate experts who helped us make good purchases—apartment buildings, single family homes, retail facilities, and the like. We were determined to not just enter into something but rather to enter into something and to do it well.

None of this should surprise you. Anything Derrick Ramsey did, he did it well. He's a helluva businessman and a great communicator. All his decisions were well thought out, meticulously investigated, and thoroughly researched. You gotta love that about a person.

Here's the deal on why things didn't go exactly as planned. We got into things at such a young age that were so advanced for people of color. We were way ahead of the curve in terms of what we envisioned in regard to syndication, retail buying, land development, and condominium conversion. We didn't have the opportunity for finance and marketing that we thought we should have had. At the time, the banks and financial institutions weren't quite ready for creative thinkers like us. They were leery of these young uppity Black guys who were moving so fast. To be honest, they were afraid of doing business with us. Getting proper backing and cashflow was always a challenge, and we ended up overextending ourselves. When the market took a hit, it was nearly impossible to recover.

Learning is a cumulative process. Much of what Derrick and I learned in football and in business, we learned together. Life is full of wonderful opportunities. There's never a time when you should forgo the opportunity to learn something new. We did that with all our real estate ventures.

I wasn't surprised at all that Derrick ended up in politics. He was always aware of what was going on in the world. He was always focused on education and providing opportunities and encouragement for young people to succeed. Playing football was just a temporary job for him. It wasn't his identity. He had far greater dreams for his mission off the field.

In life, if you always give, then you always have. I'm not talking just about money either. It's about your knowledge, wisdom, and experience also. Derrick has always had a willingness and eagerness to support and to give to the young people around him. Pay it forward and pass it on. His life has been an inspiration for so many."

Kentucky, Again

In 1994, I moved back to Lexington. My game plan at the time was to somehow reconnect with the University of Kentucky because that's what people associated me with and what they remembered me for. I always felt I would eventually make it back there at some point. My mother's health had also begun to fail around that time, and I needed to be closer to her. I didn't have any family on the West Coast, so it wasn't like there was anything holding me from moving back.

My California friends didn't think I would stay away. We were all young and still looking for excitement. They didn't think I could find enough action to keep me satisfied back in my old Kentucky home.

Even after I left Kentucky for the NFL, I maintained relationships with former Kentucky governors such as Happy Chandler and John Y. Brown. They were people who had been on a national stage and understood not only what was out there but also what Kentucky had to offer. Kentucky was a unique place, but it's a place where if you do your part, Kentucky will do its part to help you be successful. I recognized that early on.

A year earlier, I had met with UK Athletics Director C.M. Newton about possibly working as an assistant athletics director at Kentucky. He had agreed to take me on board. I told him I needed about six months to wrap up all my business deals back in California. Shortly thereafter, one of my friends—Larry Ivy—called me and told me that

Coach Newton wasn't going to be able to work out a position for me after all. They didn't have the necessary budget to swing it financially.

I understood but had already decided by then that I'd be moving back to Kentucky anyway. I still felt that in order to be successful, I had to tie myself to the university in some way.

When I returned to Lexington in February of 1994, I set up another meeting with Coach Newton. I wasn't quite sure he was the right person to address the issues on my mind. But because I knew about his background in supporting African American players everywhere he had coached, I was very direct and up front with him. I told him I had a big problem. African Americans like me could run up and down the court, up and down the football field, around the bases and the track, but we had no ability to be engaged or involved in the university's athletics programs on meaningful administrative levels.

Coach Newton was courteous and took the time to listen to everything I had to say. He told me what I said was very fair, but he never tipped his hand as to what he was thinking.

Ten or fifteen minutes after I left the meeting, I got a phone call from Coach Newton's assistant. She told me Coach Newton wanted to meet with me again right away. I turned right around and headed back to his office.

"I thought about what you said," Coach Newton said to me. "And you're absolutely right. I want you to be the face of our football program. I want you to be the announcer for UK Football."

With that, I started doing the UK Football television broadcasts with Charlie Alexander, and then later on, with Rob Bromley for the next three years. Alexander was good for me the first year because he loved to talk so much. I didn't really know how to engage and disengage as a broadcaster, so it helped me that he just talked all the damn time. Bromley and I worked great together because he knew exactly when to back out. If I pushed a little more, he'd wait until I got done, whereas Alexander would just abruptly cut me off.

Dick Gabriel, Tony Cruise, and I also did a Friday night radio call in show during football season. In addition, I also hosted the UK Football coaches show every week. Those gigs gave me plenty of public exposure over the airwaves. It provided for the perfect university tie in that I had been seeking.

The following year, I met with the university president, Dr. Charles Wethington, and he offered me a one-year trial position working for Joe Burch—a vice president for just about everything on campus. Joe was the former dean of students while I was in school. He became a great mentor and friend over the years.

By the summer of 1995, my plan was in place and working to perfection. I was Joe Burch's community relations officer. For me to be successful, I knew I had to remind people where I started—and that was at the University of Kentucky. My goal now was to build a successful bridge between the African American community and my beloved alma mater.

That goal was a lot more challenging than you may think. Even today, African Americans in Lexington are not UK fans—they're all University of Louisville fans. UK's athletic reputation has never been stellar in the minds of the Black community. Whether it's deserved or not, UK Basketball in particular has always been regarded as somewhat racist. I can't speak to it personally because all those allegations pertaining to Coach Adolph Rupp happened before I arrived. But I just know those feelings are still out there to this day.

I worked hard to create programs that would unify the local community and the university. I created a *Shadows Program* where I started bringing all these African American kids on campus to show them what UK athletics was all about. Many of these young kids lived less than two miles away. Yet they had no earthly idea where Commonwealth Stadium was located. You talk about such a massive cultural divide. I experienced so much joy exposing these kids to the university and its various athletic programs.

Not only did I bring these kids to practices and games, but I also took them into the classroom. They'd sit all bug eyed in a college classroom dreaming about someday enrolling in these same classes for real. I'm a firm believer that seeing is believing. If someone can't see themselves in class, how will they ever truly make it to class? This was my way of getting them a head start.

If you look around the country, the graduation rate for African American males is way down. I'm still trying to get UK to be fully aware of the low numbers. It's great to enroll these young men in school, but it's even more rewarding to graduate them.

In less than six months, people realized the impact my programs were making. University Chancellor Elizabeth Zinser also took note and gave me my first big university opportunity as Director of Community Relations and Fundraising for Lexington Campus. I worked with all the deans of various colleges helping them strategize their fundraising efforts. It was a huge undertaking, but one I enjoyed doing for the next three years.

Kentucky State University

During all this time, I knew I still wanted to get into athletics administration. Coach Newton and I had developed into really good friends. I picked his brain constantly and counted on him to direct my path into that specific field. I also got to know Jim Host—the sports marketing pioneer whose company at the time was broadcasting all the UK Basketball and Football games. He introduced me to a whole lot of people over the years who were instrumental to my career progression.

An athletics director wears many hats. There's the academic hat, the fundraising hat, and the public relations hat to name just a few. I had worn many of those hats during my stint in community relations. I thought I was more than ready to tackle the challenges head on.

There were two openings I felt I should explore at the time—the athletics director positions at Eastern Kentucky University and Kentucky State University. Coach Newton felt the opportunity at Kentucky State was really intriguing. Previously, the school had established a fabulous basketball tradition at the NAIA level. Before moving up to Division II, they were unstoppable in the late '60s and early '70s with stars like Travis "Machine Gun" Grant and Elmore Smith. But it was a program that hadn't won in a while, and the only direction it could go now was back up. Plus, President George Reid also coveted me as his athletics director. He put on a full court press. Although the position usually required a master's degree, he and I agreed that I could get my master's once I had gotten started. It's always nice to have the president in your corner.

I knew that if I stayed at the University of Kentucky, got my master's and possibly a doctorate, and continued to move up the ranks, I could be a vice president myself in ten years. Dr. Reid convinced me that coming to Kentucky State could potentially be a better career move. He'd give me the autonomy to build my own program the way I wanted, how I wanted, and with whom I wanted. He'd give me free rein as long as I advised him about what I was doing in case anything went awry. In his words, "we'd be in it together."

Those words were appealing to me. I knew the history of these Black colleges and what they were all about. If not for Coach Hinson taking me up to New Jersey, I would have certainly ended up at places such as Florida A&M or Grambling.

I met with Coach Newton and Jim Host about my decision. They both thought Kentucky State sounded like the right place at the right time. So, I called Dr. Reid and accepted the job offer.

I officially became the athletics director at Kentucky State University on July 1, 1999. It was a bit daunting starting out. Our football team had one winning season in the last quarter of a century. Our basketball team did well in the regular season but could never get past the first round of postseason play.

I started making changes right away with most of my focus on academics. When I arrived, our GPA was only around 2.3 for the entire athletic department. In addition, Dr. Reid also informed me during the interview process that the NCAA was investigating our program for potential violations. Thus, my first hire was a compliance officer named Tiffany Yeast (she was Tiffany Ford at the time but later married into the Yeast family of coaches). She was a former track athlete who was so helpful in getting me up to speed on all the rules and regulations.

With Dr. Reid at my side, we were able to get the NCAA violations negotiated out and any penalties put behind us. There were very few infractions once everything was all said and done. Frankly, it could have been a lot worse. There were some difficult decisions I had to make, including terminating the track coach.

When it was all over, I took a deep breath and said to myself, "So, this is how it's done."

That first year, our football team ended up around .500, but I thought they should have been a lot better. We didn't improve any the second year, so I had to make a change. We couldn't get to the next level without some new direction.

There's nothing worse than a coach who has all these fantastic plays diagrammed on the chalkboard but who can't effectively communicate the plays to his players. Such was the case with our offensive coordinator. He had all these plays written on these big old armbands that the players would wear during the games. We'd call a play from the sidelines, and the players would get all these delay of game penalties because they spent too much time looking at their armbands and trying to figure the play out. We'd go from first and goal at the five-yard line to fourth and goal from the twenty in the blink of an eye. Enough was enough. Pacing the sidelines, I was fit to be tied. I wanted the playbook to be so simple that a third grader could execute it.

Coaches have a tendency to be loyal to their existing coaches. And our head coach, George Small, just refused to part with his offensive coordinator. Since he wouldn't fire his own man, I ended up firing him and his whole damn staff at the end of the season. We couldn't afford to let one man keep the whole team from moving forward.

The interesting thing is that several years later when I was the athletics director at Coppin State, George was coaching at Florida A&M. He told me he understood why I had to do what I did. There were no hard feelings between us at all. I liked George personally. I thought he was a really good person. But you just can't be tied to a particular coach no matter how much you like him, especially when he's keeping you from winning football games.

I'm getting a little ahead of myself. Before I fired the football coach in year two, I also fired the men's basketball coach in year one. When I was hired, the basketball team would always win close to twenty games in the regular season and then get beat in the first round of the tournament. In my mind, that's a coaching problem.

So, I fired the old coach and brought in Winston Bennett as the new head coach. Winston was a well-known commodity in the commonwealth because he was a Louisville native who had starred for Joe B. Hall's Kentucky teams in the mid-1980s. I was living out in California during that time, so I didn't know much about his Kentucky career. Winston was known for his toughness and had completed recent stints as an assistant coach with the Wildcats and the Boston Celtics.

He was a great find for me. The only reason I was able to land him was because he had gotten into some trouble during his time with the Celtics. If not for that, Winston would have still been coaching in either the NBA or a Division I school somewhere. As talented as he was, I made it abundantly clear to Winston how things were going to be when you came to work for me. We had rules in place that everybody had to follow. Anybody who didn't toe the line would be packing their bags.

The first year under Winston, we won the conference, the conference tournament, and ended up in the Division II playoffs for the first time in school history. I felt I was off to a pretty good start.

That same year, our volleyball team made it all the way to the finals. During my four years at Kentucky State, our softball team also won three conference championships. We enjoyed a lot of winning success on the field.

What I was most proud of was that academically, we also lit it up. Our GPA went from 2.3 to 2.7. When you're dealing with 110 football players, that's pretty damn impressive. We also had more presidential scholars in athletics than in any other department on campus. We were flourishing all around.

This one kid named Charles Manning was like one of my sons. Charles was a senior starting point guard in my first year at K-State. Everybody loved him because he was such a nice kid. Charles was an excellent student and was getting his degree in Chemistry. That semester, he was struggling with this one class. It wasn't because of lack of effort—he just needed a little help. I told Charles I would speak to his professor and see how we could help him.

The professor was a Black guy from the Caribbean Islands who spoke with this haughty English accent. He was originally from Jamaica but—like many of his fellow countrymen—moved to England to attend college. He flat out refused to meet with Charles. He told me that where he came from, "education for athletes isn't paid for." He didn't believe in tutoring and helping "spoiled" kids.

"Here's how all this going to play out," I replied. "You're going to sit your [butt] down and meet with Charles. If not, you and I will be meeting with the president, and we'll find you some other employment where you don't have to care about kids."

He got the message immediately and soon turned into one of my biggest supporters. He ended up tutoring a lot of my student athletes. This professor was really no different than a lot of people. They had all somehow gotten the idea that athletes didn't care about education.

Nothing could be further from the truth. A recent poll asked former student athletes what one thing they would do differently if they could start all over again in their careers. Overwhelmingly, the most popular answer was that they wished they had studied harder.

The truth is that I wished I had studied harder also. Instead of getting a bachelor's degree in general studies, I wish someone had steered me toward a degree in business and economics. There simply wasn't anyone there by my side to point me in that direction. I didn't want any of my athletes to fail because no one pointed them in the right direction.

Two years into all our success, the university abruptly fired President Reid. Had he never left, I probably would have stayed at K-State much longer. The two of us were joined at the hip. After he departed, I faced several significant challenges.

The next year I had to fire Winston. He called me at home early one morning and told me he had punched a player in the face. He explained to me everything that had transpired. It was an inbounds play and the kid, for whatever reason, threw the ball right in the face of one his teammates and busted his nose. Winston immediately interceded and asked him what in the world was he doing hitting his teammate in the face. He put his hands on the kid's arm, the kid flung his hand back and hit Winston in the face, and Winston ended up clocking him.

I immediately called our new president, Dr. Bill Turner, and relayed to him all that had happened. I told him that I had no choice but to fire Winston.

Dr. Turner disagreed and wanted me to keep Winston on as coach.

"Here's what's going to happen," I informed him. "By 11:00 this morning, the press is going to be here. I'm going to tell them I'm going to fire Winston and give them the reason why. There are two policies I live by in my athletics department. Don't have romantic relationships with your students. And don't lay your hands on anybody under any circumstances."

Shortly before the press arrived, the kid Winston punched had already pressed charges. I had hoped to get in front of the situation so that I could maintain control. Now that the story was already out, however, I sent the press directly to speak with President Turner.

He still thought I was getting ahead of myself by firing Winston so abruptly.

Winston and I are still very good friends to this day. He completely understood what I had to do. He knew the rules. If you put your hands on people, then you're out. No exceptions. It was crystal clear what I had to do to maintain the integrity of my program.

Ironically, many years later, I had to dismiss Winston again when he worked for me in the Labor Cabinet. I had such a really warm feeling for him as a young brother. Because he was much more than just an employee to me, I was pissed, angry, hurt, and disappointed. You talk about a smart guy. He had so much promise. For whatever reason, he continued to make bad decisions.

After a week of President Turner and Winston going back and forth and trying to work something out, President Turner finally let him go. I had washed my hands of the whole thing by that time and was fully prepared to move forward.

By then, I had started pursuing other athletics director jobs. It was no secret that I had ambitions to become a Division I administrator. I really loved my time at K-State, though. I really loved the kids and the university itself. We were able to accomplish a lot during my four years there while I sharpened my leadership skills at a high administrative level within a well-respected organization.

My friend, Guy Morriss—the former Kentucky football coach—and I had been teammates at New England. He had recently gotten the head football coaching job at Baylor and got me in the mix for an interview for the athletics director position with the Bears. He knew how I worked and how I processed information. We felt we could work together quite effectively.

Unfortunately, I wasn't selected by Baylor and finished behind a guy who had previously been at UMass. The Minutemen had a budget of about four million dollars. My budget at K-State was about $2.5 million. Baylor University had a $14 million budget. I lost out because I supposedly hadn't managed a big enough budget. I thought that was total B.S. If I had gotten the job, I would have hired the best numbers people to manage my budget. My job was primarily to manage people—not necessarily budgets.

When I shared with Jim Host the fact that I lost out on the Baylor job because I hadn't managed a big enough budget, he suggested I come with him into state government. He had become the secretary of the Kentucky Commerce Cabinet and hoped to bring me along as his deputy secretary. As part of my official duties, I would manage the Department of Fish and Wildlife, the Kentucky Horse Park, and the Department of Human Resources—all with a combined budget of over $50 million. With that in mind, no one would be able to use "lack of budget" as an excuse against me in the future.

Kentucky Commerce Cabinet

I left Kentucky State University to become deputy secretary of the Kentucky Commerce Cabinet under Governor Ernie Fletcher in January of 2004. I had a wide range of responsibilities and oversaw a huge budget. The entire four years was an incredible experience for me. It gave me an opportunity to further sharpen my leadership skills while engaging in something totally different than what I was doing in the past. I saw firsthand how things operated at a high level in government and was able to meet directly with the governor and his executive team. Whenever Secretary Host had to miss a cabinet meeting, he would always send me in his place.

I interacted frequently with Governor Fletcher. When you're called on in those situations, you have to respond accordingly and professionally. Remember, I'm representing Mr. Host, and I certainly was not going to make him look bad. Jim trusted me and allowed me a lot of latitude when I was acting on his behalf. He put me in that position for a reason and expected me to do my job. I even got to speak on the Governor's behalf on a number of occasions as well.

I'm sure there were people who thought I was handed a lofty position in state government simply because I was a former UK athlete. Nothing could be further from the truth. Jim Host cut me no slack when I was working for him. Oftentimes I thought he was harder on me than most.

There was one instance where I was preparing some notes for Governor Fletcher prior to him speaking to the African American community. I approached Mr. Host with three or four pages of talking points I thought would help the governor. When he saw my scribblings, Mr. Host was not amused. After he had finished chastising and prodding me, my four pages of scribbling had transformed into a formal thirty-five-page speech. That was the attention to detail he expected from me.

A lot of the things I cared about, Jim cared about deeply as well. He was always on me to push my agenda harder. I kept telling him that when you stood at 6-foot-6 and 245 pounds, that was imposing enough as it was. For me to be too forceful just didn't wear well. People would shut down if they thought I was too aggressive.

I've always been big on preparation, and I've never been one to lack confidence—even when attempting something new. How many people have been in a stadium with 100,000 people looking on? As a football player, I had experienced that already. I already had a leg up on all these politicians who had never been under that kind of microscope before. I knew I could handle the pressure because of what I had previously experienced on the football field.

It's third down and one, and everybody knows you've got the ball. The eleven guys you're playing against and the hundred thousand opposing fans in the stadium are all hoping you're going to fail. And yet, you've got to make the play. Now, THAT'S pressure. It's how I've always been programmed to perform. From the time I was nine years old to the age of twenty-one, I played quarterback and was one of the best at that position. Why shouldn't I think I could excel doing what I was doing in state government?

Although many of the things I was learning about government and politics were new to me, I always tried to lead with my strengths. I took what I knew and applied it. I always tried to get my point across without yelling at people and calling them out. If there was a group, however, I wanted to be in charge. And if you're going to take charge, you had better play to win. I wanted that responsibility. Everyone who had ever been in a meeting with me knew that was my mindset.

The people I worked with took notice. When I was invited to ride in the limousine with George W. Bush during his election bid—for me to be that close to a prospective U.S. president—it demonstrated to me how highly the administration thought of me. I felt I was right on schedule to accomplish what I wanted to do with the rest of my life and my career.

During this time, Jim Host also challenged me to go and find other African Americans to work with on our team. I appointed my former teammate at Kentucky, Jerry Blanton, to serve as the deputy commissioner of Kentucky state parks. Jerry thus became the first and the youngest African American to sit in that seat. It was the highest-level position ever held by an African American in the history of our entire state parks system.

In addition to Jerry, I brought on Tiffany Yeast, my compliance person when I was at Kentucky State, as the head of human resources for the entire commerce cabinet. At that point in time, we had more African Americans serving at a director-level position or higher than any administration ever in the state of Kentucky.

It was also at this time that I finally completed my master's degree. Both my older brothers had gotten theirs many years earlier. Ty called me immediately and congratulated me. My sister also called and told me how proud she was of me. My brother Bob, however, was always a bit of a smart mouth.

"I'm not here to congratulate you," he said. "I'm going to tell you the truth. It's about time you got it done, you dumb [muthahubba]!"

Thank you, Bob.

By now you know how close our entire family was and how much our remaining family still means to me. Tragically, we lost our youngest brother, Reggie, unexpectedly in December of 2022 after he contracted double pneumonia. He was only fifty-eight years old. I had gone down to visit him in the hospital. The doctors thought he was recovering. Two days after I left to come back home, he was gone.

Prior to that in June of 2020, my sister, Joyce, passed suddenly and unexpectedly also. She went into the hospital for a kidney stone procedure and was recovering at home. The next morning, my niece found her unresponsive and rushed her back to the hospital. A couple of hours later, she was gone, having died from an infection. It's so sad.

Life is short. Savor your time with your family.

I ended up losing my mom during my time at the commerce cabinet. She was in the hospital due to heart complications, and everyone suspected that she didn't have much time left. I was so grateful that Li and I were able to spend three whole days with her before she passed.

I remember walking into her hospital room, and there she was smoking away. I told her they'd throw her out if they caught her doing that.

"I'm paying for this damn room," she shouted back to me. "So I'm going to do whatever I want in here."

Two days after Li and I left for a trip to New York, my brother called me and told me my mom had died. Because I had spent those precious days with her earlier, I was okay. I had my closure—my time with her where she and I just sat and talked. When it came down to business, I've yet to meet anyone who was any smarter than my mother. She taught me so much.

The most significant thing I accomplished during my four years as deputy secretary was being part of the team that brought in the 2010 FEI World Equestrian Games. The games come around only once every four years, and it was the first time the two-week international Olympic style event was ever held in the United States. We had gone to Bahrain for our initial meetings and personally witnessed the preceding games held in Austria, so I had a chance to discover how different organizations came together both at home and abroad.

I worked closely with John Nicholson, who was the executive director of the Kentucky Horse Park at the time, and Tandy Patrick, our chairperson. Tandy, an attorney by trade, was amazing. She had the ability to capture every single word that anybody uttered at every single meeting we attended. I told her many times that she should have been my study mate in college.

After some meticulous preparation and planning, the event went off without a hitch. So many international visitors flooded into our state and got to experience the beauty of the commonwealth and the friendliness of its citizens. They also spent a lot of money at the cash registers. The economic impact of the games was in excess of $250 million. The only thing I wasn't happy about was the fact that we were no longer a part of state government at the time. The Beshear administration got to reap all the fruits of our hard-earned labor. Unfortunately, that's the way things work in politics. Whoever's in charge at the time gets all the credit.

Ernie Fletcher's underlings ultimately killed his governorship. They became the gatekeepers and eventually made all the decisions. As a governor, you have to make so many snap decisions during the course of a day. Governor Fletcher was a very trusting guy and a very decent human being. He was a joy to work for. But he made the mistake of delegating a bit too much to those people within his inner circle who may not have had the state's best interests in mind when they acted.

Fortunately for me, they did invite me back for the World Equestrian Games' celebration. Pearse Lyons, the founder and president of the games' title sponsor, Alltech Inc., had taken a liking to me and provided me with so much encouragement and inspiration. I remember him asking me what I wanted to do with the rest of my life and challenging me to come up with ideas of going into business together.

I was honored that a brilliant entrepreneur such as Dr. Lyons thought so highly of me, but by that time I had already decided to pivot back into athletics administration. I had finally completed my master's degree and felt I had enough experience handling big budgets and managing people to be competitive for a coveted Division I slot.

I had also entertained thoughts about becoming an NFL general manager. Several years earlier—after I retired from football—I had reconnected with the Raiders' organization. I had traveled with the team to Japan on one of their occasional overseas trips. When we landed back in Los Angeles, Al Davis came up to me and told me he saw me talking to his tight ends.

"My tight end coaches make $35,000," he informed me, implying the job was mine if I wanted it.

There was no way I could survive on that salary and live in LA. Al wouldn't pay me as a player, and he still wouldn't pay me as a coach.

Several years later at John Madden's Hall of Fame induction ceremony, I spoke to Al again—not about coaching but about working in administration and perhaps one day becoming general manager of the team. At the time, Al had just hired Lane Kiffin as his new head coach. He asked me again to be his tight end coach and to meet and speak with Kiffin.

Let me just say the meeting did not go well. The guy was an arrogant jerk. There was no way in hell I was going to work for him. That was the end of that.

A year and a half or so later, I told Al once again of my interest in getting into administration. I reemphasized my desire to learn from him and to one day run the organization like he did.

I ended up interviewing not with the Raiders but for an assistant general manager position with the Arizona Cardinals. Although they decided to go in a different direction, I still felt the interview process was a valuable experience for me. Because later, I ended up circling back to interviewing for the job I really coveted—the assistant general manager position with the Raiders.

I knew I had nailed that job. By that time, Al's son—Mark Davis—had taken over for his dad and had given me his blessing. Unbeknownst to me at the time, however, Reggie McKenzie—the current Raiders general manager—had decided to hire his friend instead of me. That was a big red flag to me. It demonstrated the lack of knowledge in management within the organization at the time. Management should be hiring to their weaknesses, not based on personal relationships and networking.

Reggie hired a guy who had the exact same skill set as he did. He was a former personnel guy for the Green Bay Packers. He hired an individual who was the personnel guy for the New York Jets. He hired to his strength, not to his weakness. He basically hired himself. That was a huge mistake. I would have been the perfect guy to run the business aspect of the team because Reggie had no interest in doing that. It would have been a dream position for me. I would have worked my butt off for four or five years before going after my own team.

If I couldn't land an administrative position in the NFL, I definitely wanted to secure at least a senior associate athletics director position at a Division I school. That could then quickly lead to an athletics director position at a Mid Major program.

My friend, Tom Jurich—the athletics director at Louisville—had offered me an associate position to work with him. I turned him down because I thought if I ever stood a chance of being the athletics director at Kentucky, no way would they forgive me for having worked at Louisville. Some people thought I was crazy. I didn't think so, so I passed on that one.

Coppin State University

Then, the Coppin State job came open. Coppin State University is an HBCU located in Baltimore, Maryland. It was established in 1900 and has a current enrollment of about 2,700 students. The new president at the time, Dr. Reginald Avery, had been the academic vice president while I was at Kentucky State. He knew the way I operated and told me on several previous occasions that he liked the way I did things. He said that if he ever became a university president, he'd want me as part of his team.

In March of 2008, Dr. Avery invited me to the MEAC tournament hinting that he might be looking for a new athletics director soon. We had a great talk and enjoyed watching some exciting basketball games. A month later, he called me, informed me that he was removing his current athletics director, and invited me to apply for the position.

I applied, interviewed, got the job, and started in July of 2008. I was grateful for the opportunity but not completely satisfied with the level of the Coppin State position. The school had no football program, and I knew the measure of an athletics director was always how his school performed on the gridiron. I just believed that Coppin State was another step toward what I eventually wanted to do—a steppingstone to an athletics director position at a Power Five school.

I also knew the athletics director's success was dependent on the university president. I didn't know what my relationship was going to be with Dr. Avery. I was hoping it would be similar to the one I had with Dr. Reid at K-State. I wanted a president who was engaged, who liked athletics, and who relished the challenge of turning a program around. I wanted someone who wasn't afraid of bouncing ideas off of his subordinates and who trusted the people working under him.

Dr. Avery was all that and more. I had a great relationship with him and became familiar with his leadership style. He also let me do my own thing. Just as I did at K-State, I began traveling with the basketball team so I could get a feel for what we were doing on the road and why we were losing. It was a great way to see if the kids were disruptive in hotel rooms or whether they were making curfew. I also wanted to see how the coaches reacted when the players misbehaved. Did they go along just to get along, or did they make the changes that needed to be made? If your team's running amuck off the court, you're not going to win games on the court. Show me an undisciplined player, and I'll show you a first loser.

My parents were extremely discipline oriented. I lived through discipline as an ROTC cadet. I was disciplined as a quarterback at UK and as a tight end in the NFL. As a university administrator and as an official in state government, I always adhered to strict disciplinary rules. I wanted to win at everything I did. Without discipline, I was surely going to lose.

My basketball coach when I arrived at Coppin State was the legendary Ronald "Fang" Mitchell. He ended up coaching Coppin State for twenty-eight years, was named MEAC Coach of the Year six times during that tenure and led the Eagles to four NCAA tournament appearances. In 1997, his No. 15-seeded Coppin State team pulled a shocking upset of No. 2-seeded South Carolina in the first round of the NCAA tournament.

As great as his teams were during those previous runs, I knew I needed to make a change after the first year. My decision-making process on important matters has always been crystal clear. I'm very deliberate and calculated in my approach. Once I've made my mind up, we go with it—good, bad, or indifferent. The truth was that Mitchell's teams had become stagnant, and we simply weren't winning enough ballgames. I pleaded with President Avery to let me fire him, but he simply wouldn't allow that to happen. Of course, Coach Mitchell knew I wanted to terminate his contract, so it wasn't the best working environment for either of us.

Coach Mitchell had also served as athletics director before I arrived. He was also from Camden and knew Coach Hinson. All these factors made for an awkward relationship between us. Even though we butted heads a lot, I still had a lot of respect and admiration for what he had accomplished. My thing was wins and losses. At the end of the day, we had too many losses and not enough wins.

In his defense, it was hard to win at a place like Coppin State. My entire recruiting budget for basketball—our top sport—was $10,000. Because we didn't have very much money, those guarantee games on the road were a critical piece of my budget. We'd go on the road and play these big-name schools. In return, they'd guarantee us a substantial sum of money. The tradeoff was that you weren't going to win many of these games against the likes of Kentucky, Louisville, UConn, or Kansas. You may be $75 – 90,000 richer, but you'd leave with another loss on your coaching record.

When Coach Mitchell was athletics director, he'd personally get about twenty percent of that guarantee money in addition to his salary. Now as head coach, he was still getting those checks. I didn't think that was right. I couldn't let him keep draining money from the program simply because of the success he had earlier in his career. My responsibility was to the university who employed me. I kept appealing to the president to no avail.

Under those circumstances, I knew it was going to be hard to win athletically, so I made a conscious decision about six months into the job to focus on winning academically. If we won on the court, that would be an added bonus.

The emphasis, focus, and results paid off. In the eight years I was at Coppin State, we never had a semester where our athletics teams registered less than a 3.0 grade point average. We won numerous academic awards over that time span. One of my tennis players was the honored recipient of a coveted NCAA academic award—the first time it was ever presented to an HBCU athlete.

On top of all that, the NCAA awarded us with a $900,000 grant that allowed me to pay for summer school for all our student athletes. This money kicked me up to a whole different level. I told all my athletes that if they screwed up by not going to class or half jacking off, then they weren't getting any of this summer school tuition money.

I then put in place a mandatory ten-hour study hall for everyone. There was a lot of pushback initially, but it soon subsided. My rules, my house. If you didn't like it, you could go to school somewhere else.

I made all of my policies crystal clear—especially during the recruiting process. I'd assure all the parents of my prospective players that if their son or daughter did what I requested, I would guarantee they would graduate in four years. If on the other hand, their son or daughter didn't do what I requested, I told the parents I would call them personally to have them come down and pick them up. The parents loved hearing those words coming directly from the athletics director's mouth.

Once again, these were my rules. If a student athlete cut class, I would no longer pay for their summer school. It didn't matter whether they were academically eligible or not. If they cut class, they could foot the bill themselves.

After the first year, my athletes all bought in. I had tutors available for anyone who needed extra help. If someone was knocking it out of the ballpark academically—a 3.0 GPA or higher, doing everything I was asking them to, being respectful, representing the athletic department at a high level—I'd reward them by paying their summer school tuition.

A lot of these student athletes were already taking fifteen credit hours of classes per regular semester. They'd then tack on an additional six to nine hours during the summer. We went from athletes graduating in four years to having a bunch of them graduate in three years. Many of them would then go on to graduate school—at which time I would continue to pay their tuition if they were still participating in a sport on campus.

This was unprecedented at an HBCU. The word got around quickly. Beginning every semester, when the provost met with all the faculty members, I'd address them directly. I'd tell them exactly what I expected of them as a professor and what they could expect from me and my athletic department.

"If you have a problem with any of our athletes, call me directly," I said. "I will guarantee the problem will be taken care of."

I even offered to come and sit in on their classes. With that approach, I got all sorts of buy in from the faculty. They knew I was serious about classwork. How in the world could anyone argue against success? It seemed everyone was on board.

We went from a fifty-six percent graduation rate to an eighty-one percent rate my last year. We still couldn't compete with Morgan State or Howard University in terms of athletic budgets, but we were kicking butt academically—No. 2 in the conference to be exact. We nearly beat out Maryland Eastern Shore for the top academic honor several years in a row. My athletes were winning awards in all these academic disciplines, and I'd show up at all the ceremonies and celebrate with them.

You see, Coppin State had been around for about a hundred years, but they only had two athletes go pro in the history of the school. Academics—not athletics—was what was important to my student athletes. As our academic performance skyrocketed, pride started to creep in. We suddenly had a higher graduation rate than the University of Maryland with all their money. Howard and Hampton Universities were the mecca of HBCUs—and Coppin started kicking their butts academically also.

I ended up staying at Coppin State for eight years. That was a long time to be in a supposed steppingstone position. But that was also the amount of time needed for me to get the job done correctly. Whatever I was doing, I wanted to make an impact. And I felt I certainly made a big impact in my time at the university.

There was a Coppin State kid from Jamaica named Dale Dunn who was an Academic All-American 800-meter runner with a 4.0 GPA. One day when Dale was walking from his house to a nearby shopping center, three guys came up to him and demanded his money. Dale refused, put up a struggle, got shot, and nearly died. He remained on a ventilator in a downtown Baltimore hospital trauma center for ten days.

I visited and sat with Dale every single day he was hospitalized. When he finally regained consciousness, I told Dale I would get him anything he wanted.

"All I want is my computer," he said in a raspy voice. "I need to keep up with my classes."

Dale recovered, came back to school, and graduated early. He had another year of eligibility, so he went down to Southern Miss for his final year. He called me in January after his first semester and told me he had some bad news.

"Mr. Ramsey, I think I'm going to disappoint you," he said. "I made my first B."

The kid had made all A's his entire life. He's now a vice president for one of the Aldi food stores. I'd like to think Coppin State played a big part in his successful life story.

There was this other young lady named Ashley Bacote. Ashley was a scholarship track athlete who bombed after her first year. When she stopped going to class, I told the track coach she was out. Everyone knew my harsh stance on academics.

Ashley begged me to restore her scholarship time and time again. I wouldn't have any of it. In my mind, she had blown her chance. Her scholarship money would be better utilized by another one of her teammates who actually appreciated its value.

Ashley was persistent, however. She kept asking me for another chance, and I kept denying her request. I wasn't interested in Ashley playing me for a fool a second time. Finally, after she showed up at my office for several days in a row, I relented—but only after setting up some very strict parameters.

"3.0 every semester," I demanded. "If not, then you're out. You can still come back, but we're not paying for it."

She readily agreed, worked her tail off, and I don't think she was ever below a 3.3 GPA after that. That young gal became like my daughter. I loved her to death. She's since served a successful stint in the Navy and gotten married. Once again, I'd like to think I made a big difference in her life.

Toward the end of my Coppin State tenure, I realized I had accomplished what I had set out to do. I started interviewing for other jobs. I knew our performance on the field at Coppin could have been better, and that was probably what prevented me from landing a top position as athletics director at a big school. I'd be a finalist for everything I'd apply for, but I'd always lose out to somebody else's "guy."

For example, there was no way I shouldn't have gotten the athletics director position at Eastern Kentucky University. It was me, the assistant athletics director at the University of Washington, and another assistant AD in contention. Then along comes one of my former teammates, Steve Lochmueller, who EKU ends up hiring.

There's no way Steve's supposed to get that job before me. I'm not saying I'm that much better than him. I like him a lot as a person. It's just that here's a guy who built boats, sold cell phones, and who had never been in athletics administration before. And yet, he was somebody's "guy" because he played basketball and football for the University of Kentucky.

When I saw they were considering somebody who had absolutely no experience in leading an athletics program, I called the hiring committee and told them I was pulling out. They convinced me otherwise, and I eventually met with the president.

It was the weirdest meeting ever in that he had four or five questions for me. I answered them, we shook hands, and that was it. When I walked out of that interview, I knew I wasn't getting that job. It was completely different from the feeling I had when I interviewed previously with all his vice presidents. I walked out of those meetings *knowing I had the job*. Unfortunately for me and the other candidates, the EKU board chairman already had "his guy" in Lochmueller. They were best friends. When the board chairman's term eventually expired, EKU fired Lochmueller the next day.

By this time, I was nearing sixty. I knew I was on the short side of my career and approaching retirement age. As far as Power 5 schools were concerned, an associate AD position was probably still within reach. But I had no interest in being an associate. EKU would have been a good fit for me. I would have been back close to my Kentucky home and enjoying the conveniences of working in such familiar surroundings.

During this transition period, I also lost my dad. He had heart problems during his later years, and his heart finally gave out. My father was never the kind of person who would ever say he loved you, but there was no question that he did. He loved his entire family—he just wasn't ever one to outwardly express it. I'm so grateful for all he did for me.

6

Mr. Secretary

When the 2015 Kentucky Governor's race was going on, some of my political colleagues and co-workers from when I was deputy secretary were still in office. I reached out to them and asked them how they thought the race would play out. They hinted that the Republicans had a good chance of winning.

When Matt Bevin squeaked out the victory, I called some of my friends who knew him and asked them to see if Bevin would grant me an interview for a job in the new administration. I thought if they got me the interview, I could certainly take it home from there. I thought it made sense for me to get back into state government. But more importantly, I wanted to be closer to home.

I got an interview with the screening committee first. It consisted of about fifteen people sitting in a room firing questions at me from all angles and all sides. I later returned for a second meeting, this time with about eight people present. Once I cleared that hurdle, I got to meet directly with the governor. That first-time meeting went very well. We talked for about an hour, we discussed my philosophies, and I think Governor Bevin got a good idea of who he'd have working for him. It was obvious he had read over my resume, but I don't think deep down he really knew who I was and what I was all about.

Matt Bevin is a very smart man. During our meeting, I told him I wanted to be a cabinet secretary and explained why I would make a good one. This was a job I was thoroughly prepared for and could do if given the opportunity. I had invaluable experience as a deputy secretary in a prior administration and I had run two athletic programs where I was the final decision maker. Although we didn't discuss specific cabinet decisions, I knew a cabinet level slot was where I could be most helpful to him.

Governor Bevin seemed to agree. In a follow-up meeting, he presented me with the opportunity to run his Labor Cabinet. He made it crystal clear that he wasn't going to be holding my hand through any of this. He needed me to be a forward, out of the box thinker—essentially the CEO of the labor cabinet.

Back to State Government

What did I know about labor? Plenty. Even though I was retired from football, I was still a member of the NFL Players Association. I participated in and experienced firsthand the 1982 players' strike. I knew what unions were all about and the important roles they played in workers' lives. Despite what the skeptics said, I already understood a lot of what my new job would entail.

In 2015, Governor Bevin officially appointed me as the secretary of the Kentucky Labor Cabinet. I oversaw a budget of about $300 – 400 million. Three years later, Hal Heiner would resign, and I would then step up into the role as the Kentucky Secretary of Education and Workforce Development, with a budget of $1.4 billion. They've since combined the two cabinet positions.

I immediately began by hiring my deputy secretary and assistants. One guy—Mike Nemes—stood out. He and I hit it off right away. He was a union person and had been a union person for a lot of years. He's now gone on to become a state senator. I hired Mike to cover my weaknesses. I knew I needed somebody like him to break the ice when I went into these union halls. As you might expect, Republicans and Democrats have totally different stances when it comes to unions.

The first union meeting I went to consisted of about fifty people. I conveyed to them my stance on some key issues and told them my opinions might not always be popular with them. You see, I didn't actually care whether the people were union members or not. I didn't care whether they were Republicans or Democrats. I just cared whether they were Kentuckians and wanted them all in the workplace. My obligation was to the people of the commonwealth and to make sure that everyone was as successful as possible. No one was getting in my way.

That was something the union people weren't used to hearing, especially from a Republican administration. Usually, Republicans would enter office and beat the unions up the side of the head. My approach was different. I wanted to work with the unions. At the end of the day, if the individual worker was better off, then Kentucky was better off.

Everyone was leery at first, but they eventually came to trust me because my story and stance never changed. My parents raised me to always be truthful and to have my word as my bond. If I screwed up, I apologized. I'd own my mistakes and move on.

I can't think of any specific instances where I royally screwed up. I was a Jim Host disciple—which meant that I was always thoroughly prepared. I never went into a meeting without going over the important points a hundred and fifty times. Sure, I had the ability to speak off the cuff, but I was seldom caught off guard due to my meticulous preparation.

Don't get me wrong. I want to be crystal clear. There were some rough times throughout my tenure. For those who didn't appreciate me and what I was trying to do, I hope they've come to now understand. At the end of the day, that opportunity that I was afforded and the benefits of that opportunity over the years were way greater than anything I could have imagined. I didn't want to squander it.

I was prepared for that moment also. As a person growing up in the Deep South, I faced difficult challenges all the time. The question was: did you crumble under the pressure, or did you get stronger because of it? I got stronger. Once I started to win and more people were on my side, those pressures became just minor distractions.

The biggest challenge for me during the early years was to get the union people to truly understand our finite goals. They needed to all see the bigger picture. For example, their thoughts on the critical role of apprenticeships were totally different than what I was attempting to convey. The customary skilled unions we often hear mentioned—your pipefitters, electricians, etc.—always viewed this idea of apprenticeship as a type of watering down of their profession. Nothing could be further from the truth. I didn't want to dilute or diminish their importance. I wasn't watering anything down. I just wanted to bring their skills into the twenty-first century.

Look at the medical profession. A hundred years ago, all doctors were apprentices. Lawyers were all apprentices. What I wanted to do was to apply this concept of apprenticeship not just to the traditional skilled jobs but to all the current professions. I wanted apprenticeships in the insurance industry, in banking, in social work, state government and the like. We needed to bring everything forward in order for Kentucky to be competitive and successful.

One of the issues we have in Kentucky right now is the fact that we don't have enough skilled laborers. When outside businesses were thinking about setting up within our state, they always asked us two questions. "Do you have an educated workforce?" and "Do you have skilled laborers?" Because we always had to answer negatively to both of these queries, these businesses kept passing us over.

Thirty years ago, Kentucky, Indiana, Tennessee, and Ohio—population wise—were all within 500,000 people of each other. Fast forward to today, and Kentucky still has only 4.8 million people. Indiana now has six to seven million people, Tennessee has seven million people, and Ohio has nearly 12 million people. What have those states done that Kentucky hasn't done to grow as they did?

The answer is that they've increased their skilled laborers and grown their educated workforce. Look at our neighboring state of Tennessee. Kentucky and Tennessee are both within a day's drive of sixty-six percent of the U.S. population. Yet, Tennessee has been the one growing their workforce. Several years ago, they started an ambitious program with the goal of having sixty percent of the people earning either an associate or bachelor's degree. The campaign caught on, and businesses have since flooded into the state.

My promotion of apprenticeships was a key factor in getting Kentucky caught back up. Workers needed a defined program of classroom instruction followed by a certain number of hours of formal on-the-job training. The complexity of the specialty would dictate the length of instruction and training required to attain their certification as either a journeyman or journeywoman.

Here's the thing. Over the past fifty years, the perceived value of vocational school certification has dropped dramatically. Nowadays, everyone strives for a college diploma and a big cheesy smile instead. Society essentially told skilled workers that they weren't smart enough. What happened over time was that people promoted going to college over becoming an electrician, a mechanic, or an HVAC specialist. Subsequently, fewer and fewer people entered the skilled markets because society didn't value it by paying them proper wages.

When you ask yourself why more and more businesses are going to Mexico or China or overseas, it's because the United States now doesn't have enough skilled people to compete. When I left office in 2019, we had only about 600,000 skilled laborers total—with an average age of fifty-nine. That's not going to cut it in the competitive world market. Other developed countries with far smaller populations already have far greater numbers of skilled laborers than we do.

What I know is going to happen over the next twenty years is that the money that's going to be made is going to be made by skilled laborers. Take out the traditional high-paying professions such as medicine, law, accounting, engineering and such, and I guarantee you that skilled laborers will be making more than most everybody else. The law of supply and demand dictates their financial success. We're already seeing the shift back to skilled workers taking effect. If the United States is going to be competitive—and not dependent on other countries—this shift must continue.

If we learned anything from the recent pandemic, it's that the United States needs to manufacture its own materials. Because during Covid, smaller outside countries held us captive. We couldn't even get proper medications inside our borders. Everyday shipping issues nearly crippled our economy. We have to do better.

I knew all along that for my apprenticeship programs to ever succeed, the Commissioner of Education, Stephen Pruitt, had to endorse my ideas. Whenever I talked to school superintendents, they would always be cordial and accommodating. But they wouldn't really buy in until the commissioner gave his stamp of approval. He had to agree that we were partners—not adversaries. I finally got the commissioner to do this when he appeared on a program with me. It was a huge shot in the arm.

Another person who had the same level of passion for my apprenticeship ideas as I did was Dr. Aaron Thompson, who currently serves as the President of the Kentucky Council on Postsecondary Education. I first worked together with Aaron when he was the CPE executive vice president and provost. As African Americans, we spoke together a lot more freely about what I wanted to accomplish and how I wanted the state to benefit. Our ideas and our agendas, however, were never about us. We simply wanted to do all we could to make sure the state of Kentucky had an adequate educated workforce—particularly among the younger population.

Even today, everybody still thinks that in order to be successful, you have to be holding a college diploma. That's simply NOT true. Once I was able to get Stephen Pruitt on camera to partner with me as an advocate in these apprenticeship programs, then the support for them started rolling in. Aaron always understood the apprenticeship model and worked tirelessly with me to convey its value to others.

I mentioned earlier the Tennessee model where sixty percent of their people would have either an associate or bachelor's degree by the year 2030. I wanted to do something similar to that for the state of

Kentucky. It's great that we have all these jobs flooding into the state. But what good are they to us if we don't have anybody to fill them? When it comes to skilled laborers, there's still a big disconnect.

Dr. Aaron Thompson—*In His Own Words*

"I first met Derrick back in the '70s when I was a student at EKU and he was a student at UK. I was very aware of who he was and that he was the first Black quarterback to play football at the University of Kentucky. I followed his career closely after that but didn't really see him again until he became deputy secretary under Governor Ernie Fletcher.

We really started working together heavily when Derrick became secretary in Governor Matt Bevin's labor cabinet. At that time, we realized we had similar interests around work-based learning. When he came over into the education and workforce development cabinet, I became the president of the council on postsecondary education, and we started working arm in arm on a variety of educational and learning initiatives.

When it comes to commenting on Derrick and his leadership skills, I preface all my remarks on three particular elements. First of all, my Ph.D is in the area of reading people in organizational leadership. Secondly, as someone who carries a lot of my values on my sleeve, I can usually recognize when others are doing it also. The third element that operates between those two is being an African American male.

That smile and big presence Derrick possesses exudes confidence first of all. He's got that initial leadership look. Then when you talk with him, you get someone who's able to communicate, someone who's smart, and someone who has a definite presence. All of those qualities put together creates what I consider to be the element we recognize in someone we can follow or someone that we want to work with. Throw in the fact that he's a big guy, and that perception becomes magnified.

But Derrick also possesses sincerity. It's one thing to have bravado, but it's another thing to prove that what you say is true and that you're able to live it out. We're challenged all the time as African American men who are leaders to put up or shut up. We can't just show up and be accepted as such. I recognized that Derrick could put up as well as show up.

Confidence played a big part in Derrick's successes. When you're asked to put yourself in the center of attention, direction, and leadership—and having other people count on that—then that becomes a part of your character and your culture. All of that intertwines. Derrick's quarterbacking skills early on influenced greatly how he led, directed, showed up, and put up later in his political career. It's a growth process that he's most likely still building on.

As African American men living out our lives, we're called to represent as role models. We're living out the experience that our parents told us that we had to. My mother and father were uneducated. Derrick and I are some of the first in our families to get a college degree. Our older siblings really became role models to us as well.

Now it's also about legacy. It's not just about what we're doing currently but also about what we're leaving behind for people who might not ever meet us or know us. This is what Derrick's entire memoir is about. It's a legacy of leading and living. It's not that we do everything perfectly. Showing vulnerability is a process of leading too.

We need people like Derrick in the midst of our political system. We need honest people, not people who simply tell others that their beliefs don't matter. We need inclusive—not exclusionary—thinkers. In the old days, we called those individuals 'statesmen.' We need statesmen like Derrick Ramsey to step forward. Plus, the man looks like he's still thirty-five years old. He better have another run in him because we need him.

I've written books on student success for the past twenty-five years. One of the stronger elements of relevancy in anything you do is whether or not you're able to apply it. The reason we're losing so many young people in the workforce is that they don't understand the importance or relevance of education. Establishing workplace learning as a whole is one critical piece of the puzzle.

The other piece comes from the other end—the employer element that allows companies to mentor out and build out their workforce both for today and for the future. You can certainly do that through apprenticeships, but we wanted to take that concept to another level. There are a variety of ways we can employ apprenticeships—even in professional positions that in the past we haven't thought about as such.

The reason both Derrick and I have that common passion and desire is because we see apprenticeships as a tool that has not been utilized even a third of the way. Society still thinks of apprenticeships in old traditional ways from way back in the early days of industrialization. It's not like that at all. It's now a brand-new way of thinking about how we can use technology and artificial intelligence to better educate and expand our workforce. It's all about being relevant to the student and the employer. We're offering the student a quality experience while also offering the employer a quality employee.

Derrick has clearly been the champion of this process in his area of the workforce. I'm trying to be the champion of this in all of higher education in Kentucky.

Here's one instance where Derrick was such a valuable asset and ally for me. When I was the executive vice president and chief academic officer for higher education, I worked hard to get the original Work Ready Scholarship in place. One time, Derrick and I were on stage discussing the merits of the program. We agreed that participating in Work Ready was much more than just getting a workforce certifi-

142

cate. It was really getting an education that becomes more complete with an opportunity to think about moving into the future.

Derrick was the first workforce cabinet secretary to say that it's also something that could lead to a four-year degree—that we actually needed more baccalaureate degrees. We subsequently conjured up a way for the governor to put in an executive order to pave the way for a two-year degree that could then be stackable into a four-year degree. Since the legislature put that plan in place, it's had a huge effect on the educational attainment in our state. You can't stress how important that was.

Here's another important aspect of Derrick's tenure in government. At one point in time, the three top heads of education in the state of Kentucky were all Black men. Think about the significance of that. I was the president of the council on postsecondary education, Derrick was the secretary of education and workforce development, and Wayne Lewis was the commissioner of education.

For me, as an African American from Clay County, Kentucky—whose father was born on a sharecropper's farm—getting to the place where the three top people in Kentucky in education were all Black men is quite an accomplishment. Of course, the three of us were certainly aware of all the crap that was thrown at us simply because we were Black. But that's not what we spent most of our time focusing on. We spent our time strategizing how we could move all of Kentucky forward."

More Work to be Done

During my tenure as secretary, we also passed the *Right to Work* legislation. That was a signature bill that significantly reduced the cost of labor on major projects within the state. Artificially inflated wages were brought down to manageable levels so that these projects could proceed and be completed on time. The unions didn't like that at all, but the law made jobs much more affordable for the state. We weren't suppressing wages per se. All we were doing was eliminating all the add on costs that made projects prohibitive and that ultimately gouged the taxpayer.

Getting *Right to Work* passed was a monumental task for me. I had to travel all over the state, talk to key individuals, and secure the final votes. I even got some Democrats to cross over due to the relationships I had forged over the years with the union guys. Before, Republican secretaries never even set foot in union halls. I went to a lot of union halls in the state to build those critical relationships.

Despite the progress, I know a lot of people today are still struggling with low hourly pay. Unfortunately, I don't think it's up to me to pay them more just because I'm a nice guy. My role is to help them figure out how they can make themselves more valuable to where people have to pay them more. Hopefully, we can continue to do this through apprenticeships.

Regardless of how much an individual makes, it's also critical for people to be able to manage their income. I've seen professional athletes making hundreds of thousands of dollars a year living paycheck to paycheck because they didn't understand money management. To that effect, they were no different than the hourly worker making minimum wage.

Let me say this about Matt Bevin. I said earlier that I thought he was exceptionally intelligent. He ran a brilliant campaign to get elected, and during his first two years in office, he had a higher rating than any other governor in the country. But the guy I first went to work for and the guy I finished working for were two different people. Something made him change. You can speculate all you want on what that was.

Despite his low approval ratings, re-election was still there for the taking. We ended up losing by only 5,000 votes. Bevin, to his credit, surrounded himself with some really good people. All his cabinet secretaries were fantastic at their jobs. They were all so smart and were always trying to help each other out. When they needed to, they all stayed in their lanes. We accomplished a lot during that four-year stretch.

We brought $16 billion worth of new business into the state during his time in office. The apprenticeship programs I spearheaded were off the charts. The administration set aside $250 million to bring back those vocational schools I was advocating for. Any monies received had to be matched, so that got the communities themselves engaged in the process. The high schools, the community colleges, and the local businesses all were forced to put skin in the game—or else nobody got the money. Everybody played a part. Because of that, everybody ended up buying into the concept. Both skilled laborers and the educated workforce grew accordingly.

I knew things were working when we started not only getting young people from high school into the system, but also men and women in their forties and fifties. Life in Kentucky is better when everyone benefits. That makes me happy because I'm a proud Kentuckian. The Bluegrass state is where I've spent most of my life. I want its citizens to prosper like I did.

There were things about state government and athletics administration that were both so satisfying to my soul. On the educational front, I led the programs at two HBCUs. Remember, in 1964, my sister was the first-time college attender for our family. Fast forward to 2015—when I left Coppin State—and there were still a lot of kids who were the first-time college attenders in their families. That was so satisfying for me to help these kids—fifty years later—to have the same experience that my sister and I had.

On the governmental and political front, my last job as Secretary of Education and Workforce Development was the most satisfying job I've ever had in my life—inclusive of football. I went into communities where there was no hope and gave them hope through my apprenticeship program. The participating businesses all had agreed to pay their apprentices at least $13 an hour to begin. In two to four years, these apprentices could be making $60 – 80,000 a year. Realize the median annual income for families in Kentucky is less than $45,000. In towns with limited job opportunities, this was a valuable path towards success.

I met a gentleman who owned a company that trained people for coding procedures. That's something anyone could do remotely. Imagine how valuable an opportunity that would be for people in small eastern Kentucky communities where there are no jobs. Now they can work out of their own backyards for companies located in Washington, D.C.—or anywhere in the world for that matter. With six months of training, they could be earning $45,000 a year. If they're hard working and reliable, that figure could rise to $60 – 75,000 in another six months to a year. By bringing in opportunities like that, I was bringing in hope. That was so satisfying.

I came from a small town in Florida that for years and years never brought in any industry. They did this intentionally because they wanted to keep the wages low for the existing field workers. To this day, the only industry there is a juvenile facility. Other than that, it's still only potatoes, cabbages, cucumbers, and sod. That's not progress or hope.

To go into a community like Hastings and help someone earn a respectable living wage once they're trained up is just immensely powerful. It's empowering to give someone a resource to provide for their families. All of a sudden, they have an entirely different perspective of the world and their life in it.

I worked with a lot of good people during my time in state government. Scott Brinkman—Governor Bevin's executive cabinet secretary—was someone I wanted particularly to single out. If you're doing your work as a secretary, you know the politicians who are getting stuff done and the ones who are just along for the ride. Scott was someone who always got things done.

I always positioned myself to have relationships and conversations where there's mutual respect with those types of individuals. From the time I was labor secretary through my time in education and workforce development, I developed a very close relationship with Scott. I respected him immensely.

Jim Host told me something once that really caught me off guard. He had spoken with Scott about six to nine months after we had gotten in office. Jim's always very direct and asked Scott which secretary had been the most pleasant surprise to the governor so far.

"Well, without question, it's Derrick Ramsey," Scott replied. "I don't know if he was a surprise, we just didn't know him *THAT* way. We're just amazed at how this guy gets people to rally around him and to get decisions made."

I've said this before. All these secretaries in Governor Bevin's cabinet were good. They were really good at what they did. They all moved the ball. They all got better every day. So what Scott said about me meant a lot to me because I respected Scott so much. He was coming from a very high level. I knew the governor appreciated what I was trying to do and that it didn't go unnoticed.

Scott Brinkman—*In His Own Words*

"Derrick and I first probably crossed paths when I served in the general assembly during the Governor Ernie Fletcher administration, but we were really formally introduced during the transition period after Governor Matt Bevin's election but before he was inaugurated. I was the third appointment when Governor Bevin selected me to be the secretary of the executive cabinet, so I was involved in all the interviews with all the potential cabinet secretaries.

Of course, I was very familiar with Derrick's football career at the University of Kentucky and then in the NFL. That experience on the field transferred over to his other successes. He's a natural leader. He communicates in a way that people—his staff, people in the general assembly, people in higher education, employers—can understand. He's then able to get buy in from all the critical stakeholders.

Derrick was terrific when he took on the labor cabinet. He brought a sense of urgency to that role and had a strategic vision. He was able to develop a very good team that worked cohesively. There was never any drama with Derrick. Folks bought in to what he envisioned, and he got them to execute.

I was even more impressed when Derrick came over to the area of education and workforce development. The vision he had for the technical side of higher education—his understanding that traditional four-year colleges and universities are not for every child, that there's still a need in this country for people with the skills within the trades, and the ability to have them enter into an apprenticeship program or do a two-year certification—was clear and distinct.

These individuals could then come out of their program of study with little or no debt while making $60 – 80,000 at age twenty-one. Once again, he brought a team together that all bought in to his vision. His staff was always so loyal to him. There were never any attempts to undercut him or undermine his efforts. He was also able on so many occasions to bring on critical partners rather than to keep someone as an adversary or someone who's indifferent to his vision.

Derrick's just a high-energy guy. Once he laid out the vision and understood the compelling need to really focus on the technical side of higher education, he was just indefatigable. He reached out to employers, worked tirelessly with the community and technical college system, other community leaders, and people in the general assembly in order to get things done.

One example is how Derrick latched on to IBM's P-Tech initiative, where students earned a high school diploma, an industry-recognized associate degree, and gained relevant work experience in a growing field. He saw how something was working well outside the state of Kentucky and was committed to bringing it to the commonwealth for the next generation of children. He just went after it. When IBM wouldn't contribute money to Derrick's Kentucky initiative, he then started his own and called it K-Tech. He was absolutely relentless.

Derrick had one natural advantage that's very rare. This state bleeds blue for the most part, and Derrick was the star quarterback at the University of Kentucky. These are glory years for the state's flagship university, and there's still a very high level of regard and affection for someone like Derrick and what he accomplished during his time playing for the Wildcats. That's a nice base to build on. It wasn't so far in the past that people didn't remember how good that team was under his leadership.

But that's not nearly enough. Derrick had a vision that hadn't been previously emphasized enough. We had real gaps that needed to be addressed. It was just a coming together of a whole lot of factors that enabled Derrick to be very successful in his roles in the Bevin administration.

Governor Bevin didn't bring in politicians to run the government. He brought in smart people who had high levels of success in other fields and other endeavors. They were all good managers who weren't partisan or political. We had capable people in every cabinet who were working diligently on all sorts of initiatives. But government works slowly, and it takes time to get things done.

One of the great tragedies of Governor Bevin not getting reelected was just not having Derrick heading up another four years of a really important cabinet implementing the strategy that he laid out. It's a real crime and a tragedy for the state when the current administration just discontinued all those efforts.

The state would be very blessed if Derrick would step up and do another stint working under the next administration. We'd all be very blessed if that transpired."

Justice to Journeyman

I want people to know that there are individuals—even if I don't personally know them—who I'm cheering for. For example, people who are incarcerated occupy a special place close to my heart. My nickname in government at one point was "Second Chance Ramsey." The Kentucky prison systems weren't directly under my umbrella, but I made room for them.

I've been visiting jails for the last forty years. It tears me apart to see all these men incarcerated or caged. What pains me even more is that most of the men look like me. When the number of African American men in prison is way off the damn charts, then that becomes personal to me. I, like most African Americans, have had relatives that have been incarcerated. It's not a bad word anymore. It's just a fact of life that affects so many individuals and families.

For a person who has been incarcerated, I strongly believe that once they've served their sentence, they shouldn't have to serve time again after their release. They've already been punished through the justice system. Let's not make it harder on them when they're out. They should be able to live the rest of their lives like a normal member of society.

One of the things that always annoyed me was how once people are released from prison, society does everything they can to put them back in. There's no training program to get them accustomed to living life in a different world. If someone's been locked up for thirty years, they know nothing about cellphones, the internet, or Starbucks Coffee. And yet, in thirty days, they have to secure an ID, find a place to stay, get a job, and maintain contact with their parole officer. They have no means of transportation, so how do they do all these things?

My cabinet and the justice cabinet started a joint program called *Justice to Journeyman*. We would allow incarcerated individuals to begin their classroom instruction—and sometimes even their hands-on training—while they were still serving out their sentences. Then when they got out, they'd already have all this instructional credit and could launch immediately into the on-the-job training portion of their certification. People with successful skill sets are much more likely to become productive citizens of society.

While visiting the state of Kansas, I saw a prison program that I wanted to model and bring back to Kentucky. Incarcerated individuals there were being paid $9.50 an hour to make furniture. Part of that wage would go towards restitution, child support, or any other court-ordered payments that were part of their sentence. Anything left over, they got to save.

In addition to that benefit, they had a work release program where certain individuals who qualified could leave the jail during the day and go work. That way, they could get a jump start on becoming acclimated back into society again. The goal is to help these inmates, not to punish them further.

We tried to get a similar program implemented in western Kentucky before we left office, but the powers that be couldn't agree on enough of the specifics to get it done in time. It was hard as hell to get these politicians to buy in on something like this.

For example, there was this hard-headed senator from Northern Kentucky who I didn't like initially anyway. He was a retired cop who wore this ankle holster—essentially carrying his gun around in his sock. There's no reason to be brandishing a weapon in a public school or a state government building like that. What is he—a cowboy? That action alone just annoyed me and turned me off.

I'd tell this senator what great things we were doing with our program, and he'd accuse me of just spouting off great sound bites.

"No, Senator, it's not a sound bite," I replied to him respectfully. "And we should be embarrassed that we spend more money on the penal system than we do on education. NOW IS THAT A SOUND BITE?"

The truth is that we *SHOULD* be embarrassed. The amount of money being spent in keeping individuals incarcerated is downright sad.

Fortunately, Senate President Robert Stivers eventually helped get the final bill through and into law. In Simpson, Kentucky, certain inmates are now allowed to leave the prison at 8 a.m., go to work until 5 p.m., and get paid $19 an hour for their efforts. Remember, restitution and child support come out of that payment first. The last thing you want to happen is for these child support payments to stack up and then when the inmate is finally released, they arrest him again for not paying child support. This way, it's a win-win for everybody involved.

I can't see any reason why we can't have programs like this throughout the entire state. All employers need help acquiring workers. What our data shows is that when you give incarcerated individuals a legitimate chance to succeed, they're more reliable than the average person when it comes to work. They're getting a second chance.

I went around asking businesses to give these people that second chance. And yet, as a state, we didn't seem to be that willing to forgive. Because on the state application, there was still a question asking if someone had ever been a felon. If anyone checked "yes" on that box, you might as well toss their application in the trash. I brought that inconsistency up to Governor Bevin and he ended up "banning the box." In other words, we had that question completely removed from all state applications from that moment forward.

We also passed the expungement bill. If you were convicted of a non-violent, non-sex-related, or non-drug related offense, after five years, you could get it expunged from your record. Once again, that type of legislation helps the individual get on with their life and become a productive member of society.

These were just two more small things that we accomplished in office that ended up changing a lot of people's lives.

7

What's Next?

By December of 2019, Governor Bevin's term ended, and I had to look for a new job. I wasn't ready to retire just yet. I was so passionate about the apprenticeship programs that I signed on to do some consulting with the Urban Institute at American University. I also worked as a senior fellow for the Kentucky Community and Technical College System for a year.

That experience was frustrating for me. I worked with some really good people at KCTCS, but they didn't see my vision. That happens sometimes. Coming from Workforce and Education, I knew my finger was on the pulse. It was my fault I wasn't able to adequately convey my thoughts on jobs and education to everyone else.

We missed the mark terribly with the community and technical college systems. They were a natural progression and landing spot for my apprenticeship ideas. Had we won another term, my plan was to shift the apprenticeship programs completely over to the community and technical college system. They were already set up to train and educate folks. In my estimation, we needed another 25,000 journeymen and journeywomen in the state alone if we wanted to grow like the states around us.

Finishing Strong

I hate to keep harping on this, but lack of skilled laborers and an educated workforce were the only things keeping businesses out of Kentucky. Our state has more navigable waterways than any other state but Alaska. UPS, Amazon, and Federal Express are already in place and ready to facilitate. The state is family friendly and has a very manageable cost of living. All the essentials are already right here—except for

151

the workers.

Ford Motor Company is bringing 5,000 jobs to their new electric vehicle battery plant in Hardin County near Elizabethtown. I don't know where we're going to find the workers for it. Another business supporting the plant eventually went to Michigan instead because they knew they'd have trouble getting enough workers in Kentucky.

I don't think the current administration has the same commitment to improving the workforce like we had. I had a full commitment from Governor Bevin to go 200 miles per hour. He wanted Kentucky to be the manufacturing hub of the United States. Not everyone has to go to college to make that happen. Not every profession has to be certified in order to function effectively. We simply have to train people up properly for them to get good-paying jobs.

Places like Google and Facebook are doing just that. Our community and technical colleges are not. Instead, they're handing out certificates for simply breathing air. There's no inherent value in that. Now that's not to say all community and technical colleges are failing. I don't want to use a wide brush, but at one point we had over 106,000 students in our system. That number has plummeted to maybe 60 – 70,000. There are twenty-six well-positioned community and technical college communities in our commonwealth. There's no educational component in the state better equipped to train our workforce.

I've talked to many small business owners within the state. Many were perturbed because they were hiring graduates from all these accredited universities who didn't have the proper skills to make an immediate impact in their businesses. It would often take a year before they got any return on their investment. Large companies like Toyota could afford to provide additional on-the-job training. But for small businesses with only a few employees, you simply can't carry a person for $60,000 plus benefits unless they're productive right out of the gate.

Universities like Northern Kentucky took note. If someone had prior experience in their field, NKU would assign credit hours for that experience toward a similar career degree. What that indicated to me was that they truly understood the value of what that experience was worth in the real workplace.

I'd love it if the Republicans could return to office during the next election cycle. Then I could hopefully finish what I started. It's a shame the new regime took over. It's more than a shame because it hurts Kentucky.

Currently I serve as a board member for *Apprenticeships for America*.

152

We're lobbying hard for Congress to pass these pro apprenticeship bills. Senator Tim Scott of South Carolina has recently been a big advocate for us. Just look at industry in his state. Boeing, BMW, and Audi are all located there because of the abundance of skilled and educated laborers.

As of this writing, I'm still involved with the Urban Institute. It's another platform for me to work with politicians around the country to enhance these apprenticeship programs—particularly within our African American communities.

Bob Lerman is an Institute fellow in the Center on Labor, Human Services, and Population at the Urban Institute. The professor emeritus of economics has been writing about and promoting apprenticeships for the past forty years. He's been very helpful and insightful to me. On the topic of apprenticeships, Bob is the top authority in the country. There's no one more respected.

I got to know Bob well when I sponsored these apprenticeship seminars and invited him on as a speaker. He and I discovered that we had a lot of the same thoughts and ideas. He also serves on the *Apprenticeship for America* board with me.

There were two kids working for a small company in Louisville manufacturing machine parts who became the models for what Bob and I were trying to demonstrate through our apprenticeship programs. Both were enrolled in the Speed School of Engineering at the University of Louisville but left to work for this company fixing machinery. It took them three years to achieve journeyman status. In year five, they were already making six figures—with no educational debt. This was by far the best career path for them.

Bob not only has all this understanding, but because he's a researcher, he also has all the data. When I was Education and Workforce Secretary, I leaned heavily on that data to convince my fellow cabinet heads that apprenticeships were the key to increasing the workforce. Out of the corners of my eye, I'd always notice the snickers in the room when I rattled off the numbers. Remember, as a former quarterback, I had excellent peripheral vision.

I believed in those numbers, and all my colleagues eventually came around to believing them too. I knew I had gotten my point across when the secretary of Information Technology asked me how he could find some trained workers for his staff. In order to work in IT for the state of Kentucky, you had to have a bachelor's degree. There simply weren't enough people with degrees to fill the slots. But any person with half a mind knows that you don't have to have a college degree to work in IT. The average high school kid could do more in that field than most of us with advanced degrees. In situations like this, we brought people on as apprentices, and it became a win-win for everyone.

We also helped find social workers for the state in the same manner. Most of these workers were college students hired on part time. They were in school getting their degrees while also getting some practical experience and a paycheck to boot.

We were able to finally accomplish what Bob had been promoting all these years. Even the *New York Times* picked up on all the great things we were able to do with apprenticeship in Kentucky state government.

I'm also working hard at this time on the concept of housing vouchers. All the data shows that the fastest and best way to wealth is through home ownership. When the interest rates dipped below two and three percent, it was cheaper for people to own homes than to rent. We wanted to get the home ownership process started for the lower income communities in our country. Not just the African American communities mind you, but all lower income individuals. Poverty doesn't discriminate. It has no color. It's satisfying watching families at all income levels fulfill their American dreams.

University of Kentucky Board of Trustees

During my time as education secretary, I approached Governor Bevin telling him of my desire to be on the UK Board of Trustees. Having gone to school at Kentucky—and having gone to work at the university as well—I thought I had a lot to offer. I had a true understanding as both a student and as an employee of the challenges involved. It was a different perspective in which I'd hopefully bring some different ideas and approaches because of my unique experiences.

The UK Board of Trustees is the final authority in all matters affecting the University. It exercises jurisdiction over the University's financial, educational, and other policies and its relation with state and federal governments. The Board consists of sixteen members appointed by the Governor serving six-year terms, two members of the UK faculty, one University staff employee, and one member of the student body.

Not only did I go to school and work at UK, but me being African

American and also in higher education only added to my desire to serve. I understood the role the University should be playing in getting the workforce prepared for potential businesses coming to the state.

When businesses came in to visit with the state's economic development leaders, I would sit in on most of those meetings. I knew exactly what kinds of workers they were looking for and what the trends were in terms of jobs and hiring. I knew all the relevant numbers and statistics already. My job as education and workforce secretary gave me natural insights as to how I needed to perform as a board member.

The university president answers to the Board of Trustees. Dr. Otis Singletary was the president during my playing days and ended up being a dear friend and one of my biggest supporters. He and I maintained a great relationship until his death in 2003. Dr. Charles Wethington was the UK president when I was first hired back in 1995, and I remained very friendly with him.

I first met current UK President Eli Capilouto down at the Final Four in New Orleans in 2012. I was athletics director at Coppin State at the time. I was walking down Bourbon Street, and someone pointed him out to me. I went up and introduced myself, and we agreed to meet whenever I returned to Lexington. A couple of years later, we did meet and have since developed a solid relationship.

Dr. Capilouto has been a very good leader. He understands the big picture. Sometimes I think leaders get pigeonholed and they can only see the immediate perspective in front of them. Dr. Capilouto understands the entire organization. He's hired good people to help him run it. But most importantly, he has a good understanding of the university's role within the state.

I believe that anytime somebody is on a board, they should be a contributor and not just a "seat warmer." I made darned sure my views were known to everyone—including Dr. Capilouto. I'm a big-picture guy as well, so I'm also always looking at the obligation the university has to the Commonwealth.

Just like every other aspect of my life, I came into our board meetings prepared. I had no problem asking hard questions, having honest conversations, and speaking my mind freely with other board members. Oftentimes my thoughts and ideas were different. Some of them may have even been thought of as radical. Well, if the betterment of the university I love is considered radical, then so be it.

One of the topics I was always super sensitive about was the cost of a college education. If not for my athletic scholarship, I would not have been able to attend college. Our family simply couldn't afford it. Therefore, I was always keyed in to discussions about raising tuition. I watched those rates very closely. Tuition rates have risen at Kentucky, but not to the extent they could have or that they have at other schools.

I was also very sensitive to graduation rates. What good does it do when someone attends your school but doesn't graduate? They leave with no degree and a whole lot of debt. I was particularly sensitive to the plight of the African American male student. Low graduation rates of African American males at both historically White and Black institutions have been especially troubling to me. It's something I also paid very close attention to during my time on the Board.

A lot of construction went on during my tenure. Be it athletics or academics, students nowadays are attracted to shiny new objects. When young people tour campuses, they want to see new buildings with all the bells and whistles utilizing the latest advances in science and technology. Just like in the sporting world, I likened recruitment on campus to an arms race. The person who has the most stuff attracts the best athletes.

Not only did we need to spend money to attract students, but we also wanted to leverage our athletics reputation. People know about Kentucky Basketball on the moon—it's been THAT good for THAT long. On the football side, Kentucky is in the Southeastern Conference—where the majority of national championships teams seem to reside. It's no secret that athletics is an important component of the university as a whole. Athletics Director Mitch Barnhart came to every one of our quarterly board meetings and told us what and how his department was doing. Again, I look hard at graduation rates, and in that regard, Mitch has done a very good job.

Not surprisingly, my biggest impact on the board has been in the area of workforce development. Right from the outset, I wanted desperately to get the university presidents to understand that student success involved much more than just getting a glorified college diploma. College presidents and faculty think they have all the answers. They've supposedly been doing this education thing for the last twelve hundred years. Of course they know education.

But what they didn't know was that the world was changing. What the businesspeople were telling me loud and clear was that the graduates coming to work for them with these fancy college degrees were no help at all to their companies. We needed to find a way to get them some practical hands-on work experience as part of their degrees.

This concept was a hard sell from the very beginning. No one wanted to do any sort of internship or apprenticeship while they were getting a degree at the University of Kentucky. Yet, the reality was that Kentucky hovered around forty-eight out of all the fifty states in terms of workforce participation. At its peak, only fifty-eight percent of Kentucky's 18 – 64 population was in the active workforce. The national average is sixty-three percent. If you want to be a top-25 university in the country, you can't be ranked near the bottom like that. Your graduates need to be better prepared.

To Dr. Capilouto's credit, he listened to me and to what the employers out there were saying about the university's graduates. We have to find ways to get them more work-related experience and to grant them proper college credit for that experience. We still have a long way to go, but at least colleges seem to be much more receptive now to the ideas that I've been harping on. On this topic, they know I'm right.

I stayed off of the athletic committee by design, and pretty much chose to serve on the academic, the finance, and the audit committees instead. I worked with some really smart people who committed their time and expertise to serving together with me. None of us were paid a dime. Although we only officially convened face-to-face four times a year, we were constantly in touch with each other discussing topics through phone calls, emails, and texts. We had a common goal in making the University of Kentucky the best it could be for the citizens of the state.

My time on the Board was more than gratifying. It gave me another snapshot of my relationship with the school and the state. When you attend as a student, you have no idea of what the higher-ups are doing or how they're doing it. They make decisions and you just follow along. When you work here, you start to understand a little bit more of what's going on at the decision-making levels. When I worked for the university, I was in fundraising and community service. So, I got to understand the inner workings of the university in those two particular areas. Then, as a board member and as education and workforce secretary, I was able to view the university from all different angles and fully understood its complete role within the state.

Remember, I'm a big-picture guy. Oftentimes, you need experience and perspective to fully understand the big-picture issues.

Epilogue

By now you know that I came from very modest means. I'm proud of where I came from. I'm also proud of what I've been able to achieve since those humble beginnings.

I love Kentucky. There's no place like my old Kentucky home. I remember a conversation with the great Cawood Ledford—the iconic radio voice of the Wildcats—about why he never left the state.

"This is my home, and I love being home," Cawood said. "The people of Kentucky will always take care of me, so I don't ever need to leave. I get to stay around people that I like while living the life that I enjoy."

This state has given me opportunities I never would have imagined. My parents taught me to dream big, but my dreams were never this big. I've been given opportunities and access to people who could make a difference in our state, our country, and our world. I'm not bragging, but there's not a politician, executive, or community leader I can't touch. I've worked my way to the table for that privilege. Now I'm trying to pay it forward.

These folks that are incarcerated, poor folks in Eastern Kentucky, folks struggling to make ends meet in the large urban areas of Louisville—I'm cheering for all of them. I'm cheering for them to have the same life and opportunities I've had. I'm cheering for them to have the same success I've enjoyed. They need to understand that I'm cheering and praying for them even though I don't know them personally.

I am so grateful. For the rest of my life, I'm trying to help whomever I can because so many people—even the ones I didn't know—have allowed me to stand on their shoulders during my journey.

I remember my meetings with Governor Happy Chandler. He's someone else who took a liking to me for whatever reason. We would meet at Mama Royal's Café, which was a trailer on Loudon Avenue, and have conversations about how Derrick Ramsey should conduct himself. He referred to me both as "Sonny Boy" and "The Chosen One."

One conversation we had that I'll never forget was about Jackie Robinson, who broke the Major League Baseball color barrier when Happy Chandler served as commissioner. Jackie wasn't the best African

American player at the time. Satchel Paige was the guy back then. Or Josh Gibson. Why was Robinson chosen over them?

"If I had chosen Satchel Paige," Governor Chandler answered. "He would have set your people back twenty-five years. He was a drinker and a womanizer and a man about town."

I responded by telling Governor Chandler that no one was more of a drinker and womanizer than the great Babe Ruth.

"Yeah, but Babe Ruth was White," Governor Chandler replied.

He then brought the conversation back around to me.

"At the end of the day, people decide who they want to follow," he continued. "It appears that everybody wants to follow you. Once they decide to follow you, you have to deliver for them. You can't be out there drinking in public, getting in trouble, and running to the bars. Every time you take the field, you're out there for every African American in the state of Kentucky."

That bothered me a bit. I didn't come to Kentucky to be Dr. Martin Luther King Jr. I came to get an education and to get to the NFL. In retrospect, what Governor Chandler said was right on target. But at nineteen years old, it was a little more than what I could grasp at the time I heard it.

Fast forward to my time as deputy secretary. I'm traveling to all these counties within the state and meeting with African Americans in their seventies and eighties. I'd introduce myself to them, and they'd all tell me that they knew exactly who I was. They had pulled for me during my time playing football. But they said they didn't pull for UK. They pulled directly and specifically for me.

What Happy Chandler told me twenty-five years earlier was so right. Every time I took the field, I was playing for every African American in the state of Kentucky. A lot of those folks didn't have the opportunities that I was given. I was playing for their vision, their hopes, and their dreams. I couldn't afford to fail.

For every young African American boy out there—I don't care where you are—I want you to know that you have a chance to be bigger and better than me. I want every Black kid, every poor kid, every kid growing up in a broken home to realize that the sky is the limit. And the only thing that limits you is when you don't go after what you want—when you don't pursue your dreams.

My name is Derrick Ramsey. They call me Mr. Secretary.

Dr. John Huang—*In His Own Words*

It's been a while—nearly fifty years in fact—since I sat in the stands at Commonwealth Stadium watching a young Derrick Ramsey leading the Wildcats through that magical 1977 football season. Even back then, Derrick was the anointed one in my mind—the quarterback and unmistakable team leader propelling his teammates to an unprecedented 10 – 1 record and a No. 6 national ranking.

To be honest, I never viewed Derrick as strictly a Black quarterback. His skin color was inconsequential to me. In fact, I don't even remember the home fans booing him during the game against West Virginia. As a pre-dental student, perhaps I was way too focused on just surviving organic chemistry to even notice the poison arrow of racism rearing its ugly head. It's only with the benefit of hindsight that I've come to really appreciate Derrick, what he went through, and all that he's achieved in his life so far.

Put simply, Derrick Ramsey remains the most accomplished athlete in University of Kentucky Athletics history. I'm not just talking about on the field—although an argument can certainly be made for leading the team to an undefeated SEC record and a ten-win season in a year without a bowl game (a feat that hasn't been duplicated since and probably never will be). Add in his accomplishments after he left UK—performing at the highest levels in the NFL, in athletics administration, and in state government—and you'd be hard pressed to find many others with a resume to match.

Jamal Mashburn, with all his business successes, perhaps? Or maybe Pat Riley, with what he's done as a championship level coach and in the front office of the NBA? Sure, there've been other UK greats who went on to have successful careers outside of their respective sports. But only a select few have had the impact upon the collective people of the commonwealth that Derrick has had in his lifetime.

The challenge in telling his story, then, was to properly capture that impact and have it resonate boldly and loudly throughout the narrative. We hope we've done that through the chapters you've just read. The racial overtones ring loud and true, but we didn't want that element to overshadow the main message: that regardless of your pedigree or lot in life—if you work hard enough—your dreams can come true.

Ultimately, They Call Me Mr. Secretary, is a motivational story—a tale of how an African American kid growing up in Hastings, Florida, worked his way up to a seat at the table and made a difference in those around him. I found Derrick's story intriguing and engrossing. I hope you enjoyed reading it as much as he and I enjoyed telling it to you.

One of my favorites parts of doing a book project like this is diving deep into the subjects involved. Derrick did not disappoint. Prior to working together, we had never met. Of course, I knew about him and all his wonderful exploits. I just didn't know him—how he thought and what made him tick. I also wasn't aware of how smart, personable, and engaging he was. Or how much he cared about Kentucky—the state he now calls home.

The reality is that you can't sit through hours and hours of conversations with someone without getting to know them intimately. I'm honored to have been given that opportunity with Derrick. It's been a privilege being able to pick his brain about politics, religion, family, sports, government, or whatever else tickled our fancy at the moment. I'm blessed to have been let into his private inner circle to talk to all who have helped him along on his journey.

Life is all about relationships. And it's about giving back and paying it forward. It's about taking all your God-given abilities to make the world a better place. No one has done that better than Derrick.

I'm blessed to call him my friend.

I'm honored to call him Mr. Secretary.

About the Authors

Derrick Ramsey was the first African American starting quarterback in the history of the University of Kentucky football program. In 1977, the first-team All-Southeastern Conference and third-team All-American captained the Wildcats to an unprecedented 10 – 1 season and a No. 6 national ranking.

Prior to Kentucky, Ramsey—a native of Hastings, Florida—won two state high school football championships in the Sunshine State before finishing up his prep career in Camden, New Jersey. In his senior season, he led Camden High to another state football title while also adding the school's first basketball state championship to his many athletic accomplishments.

After graduating from Kentucky, Ramsey went on to have a successful nine-year NFL career, including winning a 1981 Super Bowl ring with the Oakland Raiders and twice becoming a Pro Bowl first alternate. Upon retirement from football, a burgeoning entrepreneurial spirit led Ramsey into real estate management as a small business owner in the Bay Area for several years. Knowing he wanted to reconnect with his Kentucky roots, Ramsey returned to his alma mater in 1994 as the school's Community Relations Officer.

In 1999, Ramsey became the athletics director for Kentucky State University. By creating an innovative Student Athlete Excellence in Academics Program, he helped the university's athletic department produce more Presidential Scholars than any other department on campus.

In 2004, Ramsey was appointed Deputy Secretary of Commerce in Governor Ernie Fletcher's administration. While in that role, he oversaw a $50 million budget and was part of a key delegation that successfully brought the renowned 2010 World Equestrian Games to Kentucky and to the United States for the first time ever.

After leaving office in 2008, Ramsey returned to athletics administration as the athletics director at Coppin State University. For the next seven years, he led the Baltimore HBCU's athletic department to unprecedented levels of academic achievement.

In December of 2015, newly elected Kentucky Governor Matt Bevin called on Ramsey's proven track record in administration and state government by asking him to once again serve the citizens of the Commonwealth, this time as Secretary of the Kentucky Labor Cabinet. In 2018, Governor Bevin then appointed Ramsey as Secretary of Education and Workforce Development, a position where Ramsey worked passionately and tirelessly for all workers residing within the state.

As of this writing, Ramsey has just completed a six-year term on the University of Kentucky Board of Trustees.

He and his wife, Jalica (Li) live in Lexington.

Dr. John Huang is a retired orthodontist, military veteran, and award-winning author. He currently serves as a freelance reporter and sports columnist. He is the author/coauthor of four other books, *Cut To The Chase, Kentucky Passion, From The Rafters Of Rupp, and Serving Up Winners*. You can contact him at www.Huangswhinings.com or follow him on social media @KYHuangs.

Made in the USA
Las Vegas, NV
13 December 2023

82638236R00098